Vegetarian 101

Cover photo © Brave New Pictures.

Food Stylist: Mary Valentin

Photos on the following pages from Shutterstock: 4, 10, 13, 16, 17, 18, 19, 20, 24, 34, 48, 62, 78, 96, 127, 130.

Photos on the following pages from Brave New Pictures: 29, 41, 55, 59, 83, 91, 105, 110, 119, 137, 147.

Printed in China.

Library of Congress Cataloging-in-Publication Data

Vegetarian 101 : master vegetarian cooking with 101 great recipes / edited by Perrin Davis.

   p. cm.

Includes index.

ISBN-13: 978-1-57284-132-1 (flexibound)

ISBN-10: 1-57284-132-X (flexibound)

ISBN-13: 978-1-57284-698-2 (ebook)

ISBN-10: 1-57284-698-4 (ebook)

1.   Vegetarian cooking. 2.   Cookbooks. I. Davis, Perrin, 1969- II. Title: Vegetarian one hundred one. III. Title: Vegetarian one hundred and one.

TX837.V42286 2012

641.5'636--dc23

2011042636

10 9 8 7 6 5 4 3 2 1   15 14 13 12

Surrey Books is an imprint of Agate Publishing, Inc.

Agate and Surrey books are available in bulk at discount prices. For more information, go to agatepublishing.com.

Vegetarian 101

MASTER VEGETARIAN COOKING WITH 101 GREAT RECIPES

EDITED BY Perrin Davis

S

SURREY
BOOKS

AN AGATE IMPRINT

CHICAGO

CONTENTS

INTRODUCTION

**A**gate Surrey Books wants to help everyone, but especially kitchen beginners, learn how to explore different kinds of food and cooking. We are proud to introduce the *101* series, which aims to provide rewarding, successful, and fun cooking experiences for everyone, from novices to more experienced cooks. *Vegetarian 101: Master Vegetarian Cooking with 101 Great Recipes* is one of the first books in this series, and it offers readers not only delicious recipes but also useful information about shopping for equipment, ingredients, kitchen essentials, and seasonings. Getting started with vegetarian cooking can be intimidating, but we'll demystify the process for you. So whether you or someone you love just recently adopted a vegetarian lifestyle, or if you have been a vegetarian for some time now, *Vegetarian 101* is a great place to start.

Most of the recipes in these *101* series books come from a wide range of Agate Surrey authors and editors. Contributors to *Vegetarian 101* include Sue Spitler, editor of the "1,001" series that includes such titles as *1,001 Low-Fat Vegetarian Recipes*, and Barbara Grunes, author of *Diabetes Snacks, Treats, and Easy Eats: 130 Recipes You'll Make Again and Again* and *Diabetes Snacks, Treats, and Easy Eats for Kids: 130 Recipes for the Foods Kids Really Like to Eat*.

Vegetarian 101 recipes were selected to provide a starting point for anyone beginning their vegetarian-cooking journey. The collection includes a variety of cuisines (Italian, Mexican, Spanish, French, Middle Eastern, and Asian, to name a few). Most of the recipes are simple, although a handful of them are more advanced; you'll find that all are easy to follow.

A TASTE OF WHAT YOU'LL FIND IN THIS BOOK

This book contains lots of fantastic main-dish options in the Salads and Entrées chapters. Don't miss great dinner-party options like Shells Stuffed with Spinach and Tofu; Orecchiette with Artichoke Hearts, Mushrooms, and Peppers; Porcini Risotto; and Eggplant Provençal, as well as delicious family pleasers like Tacos

Picadillos and Bourbon Street Red Beans and Rice. Black Bean and Smoked Tofu Salad and Falafel Pitas with Tahini Dressing will put smiles on everyone's face, and Cranberry Cheese Melts are a big favorite in our house.

In the Side Dishes chapter, check out delicious dishes like Veggie-Stuffed Bakers, Creamed Spinach, Orange Cilantro Rice, and Polenta.

Looking for a delightful bread option to serve with dinner? Try the Roasted Red Pepper Bread or the Queenly Quinoa Crackers! Glazed Chocolate Shortbread Squares, Chocolate–Cherry Pudding Cake, and Pineapple-Lemon Trifle are just a few of the tasty offerings in the Desserts chapter. Need to delight a more sophisticated palate? Look no further than our Chocolate Phyllo Cheesecake on page 146.

But before you get started cooking some of these great recipes, make sure you're up to speed on some vegetarian cooking basics, and that your kitchen and pantry are ready to go!

VEGETARIAN COOKING BASICS

Eating vegetarian is extremely healthy. Medical research increasingly supports the health benefits of increasing the amounts of fruits, vegetables, grains, beans, breads, cereals, and pasta in our diets and limiting, if not totally eliminating, meat, poultry, fish, dairy foods, and fats.

A vegetarian diet consists of food that does not include meat, but there are many different kinds of vegetarian diets. Vegan diets exclude all meat, dairy, eggs, cheese, butter, and even honey. Ovo vegetarian diets include products made with eggs; lacto vegetarian diets include products made with dairy products; and lacto-ovo diets include foods that contain both dairy and egg products. Pescatarians eat no meat or poultry, but they do indulge in fish and seafood (none of the recipes in this book contain fish or products derived from fish). You'll see that the recipes in this book are labeled according to whether they are vegan, lacto, ovo, or lacto-ovo vegetarian.

A vegetarian diet is mostly based on fruits, vegetables, grains, beans, and legumes. Vegan recipes also often include soy dairy alternatives, meat substitutes, and other vegan products. Cooking vegetarian and vegan fare, both at home and in restaurants, is one of the fastest-growing food trends in the United States

It's commonly thought that vegetarian cooking is high in fat, due to ingredients such as nuts, cheese, or oil that are included as meat substitutes and for flavor and nutrition. We've proven here that vegetarian cooking *can* be low in fat without losing a bit of delicious flavor. To achieve optimal nutrition, we emphasize the use of fresh versus processed ingredients and use the many excellent reduced-fat and reduced-sodium products currently available. Flavors are fresh, with an integrity further enhanced by herbs and seasonings.

KITCHEN EQUIPMENT BASICS

If you are a new cook, or it's been a while since you've spent time in the kitchen, here is some helpful information that will make it easy to jump into *Vegetarian 101* recipes. The following is not necessarily vegetarian-cooking specific, but if you have the following equipment, you will be prepared to make almost any recipe in this book.

Appliances

We're sure you know this already, but your kitchen should include the following standard set of appliances.

Pretty Much Mandatory

- Refrigerator/freezer (set to about 34°F to 38°F [1°C to 3°C], or as cold as you can get it without freezing vegetables or drinks)

- Freezer (if yours is not frost-free, you'll periodically need to unplug it to defrost your snow-filled box)

- Stove/oven (make sure to keep the oven very clean, as burnt foods and other odors can affect the taste of your food)

- Microwave (again, make sure it's clean and ready for use), because it's great for defrosting

- Blender (and not just for beverages and soups—you can use it in place of a food processor or an immersion blender in some instances)

- Hand mixer (you can always stir by hand, but sometimes, the hand mixer is indispensable)

Optional

- Food processor
- Immersion blender
- Stand mixer
- Slow cooker

Pots and Pans

The following are useful basic equipment for any kitchen.

- Stockpot (8 to 10 quarts [7.6 to 9.5 L])
- Dutch oven (5 to 6 quarts [4.7 to 5.7 L])
- Pancake griddle
- Large stockpot with lid (6 to 8 quarts [5.7 to 7.6 L])

- Large skillet with lid
  (10 to 12 inches in
  diameter [25 to 30 cm])

- Medium skillet with lid
  (7 to 8 inches in diameter
  [17.5 to 20 cm])

- Medium and large saucepans with lids (2 and 3 quarts
  [1.9 to 2.8 L])

- Small saucepan with lid (1 quart [.95 L])

- Glass casserole dish (2 quarts [1.9 L])

- Square cake pan (8 or 9 inches [20 to 22.5 cm])

- Rectangular cake pan (13 by 9 inches [32.5 by 22.5 cm])

- 2 loaf pans (8 inches [20 cm] long)

- Muffin pan (12 muffins)

- Pie pan (9 inches in diameter [22.5 cm])

- 2 baking sheets

General Utensils

These are recommended
basics for any kitchen.

- Knives: Chef's knife, serrated
  knife, and paring knife

- Measuring cups for both
  dry and liquid measures

- Measuring spoons

- Mixing bowls (two or three,
  ranging from 1 or 2 quarts to
  5 or 6 quarts [.95 or 1.9 L to 4.7 or 5.7 L])

- Wooden spoons, slotted spoon, rubber or silicone spatula, ladle, whisk, tongs, and a large metal "flipper" for veggie burgers and similar foods

- Colander

- Cheese grater

- Citrus zester

- Salt and pepper mills

- Kitchen scissors

- Vegetable peeler

- Can opener

- Cooling rack

- Kitchen timer

- Cutting boards

- Pot holders

- Kitchen towels

Storage and Paper Supplies

Either in a handy drawer or on a shelf, make sure you have all of these items within easy reach.

- Plastic or glass storage containers (5 to 10, varying sizes)

- Aluminum foil

- Plastic wrap

- Parchment paper

- Small zip-top bags

- Large zip-top bags

- Muffin cup liners

BASIC INGREDIENTS LIST FOR VEGETARIAN COOKING

This section includes the basics that you should have on hand, but this is by no means a comprehensive list for every recipe in this book. If you have these ingredients as a starting point, however, you'll be in great shape to tackle almost any of the *Vegetarian 101* recipes!

Seasonings and Flavorings

- Bay leaves
- Cayenne pepper
- Chili powder
- Ground cumin
- Dry mustard
- Garlic powder
- Ground cinnamon
- Ground ginger
- Ground nutmeg
- Red pepper flakes
- Rosemary
- Basil
- Oregano
- Paprika
- Kosher salt
- Vanilla extract
- White pepper
- Freshly ground black pepper
- Vegetable bouillon cubes or base (just add water to make instant stock)

Condiments

- Apple cider vinegar
- Balsamic vinegar
- Honey
- Hot pepper sauce
- Ketchup
- Mustard
- Olive oil
- Red wine vinegar
- Rice vinegar
- Soy sauce
- Vegetable oil
- White wine vinegar

Baking

- Corn starch
- Baking powder
- Baking soda
- Butter or margarine
- Vegetable shortening
- 2% or skim milk
- Maple syrup
- Molasses
- Granulated sugar
- Light brown sugar
- Unbleached all-purpose flour

- Unbleached whole wheat flour
- Unbleached white spelt flour
- Dutch process cocoa powder
- Fresh large eggs or egg substitute

General

- White or brown rice
- Garlic
- Semolina or whole wheat pasta
- Onions
- Canned tomatoes
- Lentils
- Raisins
- Tomato sauce
- Vegetable broth

COMMON COOKING TERMS

You probably are quite familiar with most of these terms. If this is your first time cooking or it's been a while since you've been in the kitchen, here is a quick refresher:

- **Bake:** To cook food with dry heat, usually in the oven at a specified temperature.

- **Boil:** To cook food in boiling water (212°F [100°C]) on the stovetop.

- **Blanch:** A technique that involves immersing food in boiling water for a brief period of time and then immediately transferring into an ice bath in order to stop the cooking process. Blanching is an excellent technique for quickly cooking tender vegetables, as it helps them retain their firmness, crispness, and color.

- **Braise:** This technique is a combination of browning the surface of a meat substitute, which means to cook the meat substitute at a high temperature for a short amount of time, followed by cooking at a lower temperature in a covered pot with liquid for a longer period of time.

- **Broil:** To cook over a high heat at a specified distance from the heat source, usually in the oven or in the "broiler" part of the oven.

- **Deep fry:** To cook food by immersing it in preheated oil.

- **Grill:** To cook over an open flame on a metal framework, grid, or other cooking surface.

- **Roast:** To cook food in an oven in an uncovered dish, usually resulting in a well-browned surface that seals in juices and flavors.

- **Sauté:** To cook food over a medium-high or high heat in a skillet or sauté pan in a small amount of oil, water, stock, or other liquid.

- **Steam:** To cook food with steam, usually in a steamer rack or basket positioned over (but not immersed in) a pan containing a small amount of water.

- **Stir-fry:** To cook over high heat with a small amount of oil; usually requires regular stirring as food is cooking. It can be used for several kinds of dishes and is often associated with Asian fare.

GENERAL COOKING TIPS

No matter what you're cooking or how many people you're serving, a few universal rules of the kitchen will make your life easier. The following is a list of our recommendations for the novice cook. These great habits will ensure fewer mistakes, less stress, and ultimately more delicious food.

- **Read every recipe from beginning to end, at least twice, before you start cooking.** This will help to ensure that you understand how it should be made and what you need to make it.

- **Set up your ingredients, pots, pans, and utensils before you begin to prepare the recipes.** We never start a recipe until we have every ingredient on the counter in front of us. (If possible, we also premeasure all the ingredients and have them ready to add, because there's nothing worse than accidentally dumping half a box of kosher salt into an almost-finished recipe.) If you know you'll need a greased pan in step 4, grease it and set it aside before you even get started.

- **Keep a grocery list and a pen attached to the refrigerator.** If you go to the grocery store without a specific list of what you need, you're likely to forget at least a few items.

- **Clean up as you go.** If you take the time to clean your dishes as you're cooking, you'll find that you will have more space to work in and less to do after the meal is done.

- **Time the meal.** It can be complicated to cook multiple recipes at once and make sure that everything ends up finishing at roughly the same time. Make sure you allow for enough time for everything to get done, and for recipes to be cooked simultaneously.

- **Be careful.** It sounds silly, but never forget that you're working with high-temperature appliances and cookware and sharp utensils! Use proper precaution when lifting lids, turning pans, and straining vegetables.

- **Have fun!** We hope you enjoy learning how to cook these recipes and sharing them with others.

APPETIZERS AND DIPS

BAKED ARTICHOKE DIP (LACTO-OVO)

Everyone's favorite!

16 SERVINGS (ABOUT 3 TABLESPOONS EACH [45 ML])

> 1 can (15 ounces [426 g]) artichoke hearts, rinsed, drained
> ½ package (8-ounce [227-g] size) Neufchatel or cream cheese, softened
> ½ cup (45 g) grated Parmesan cheese
> ½ cup (119 mL) reduced-fat mayonnaise
> ½ cup (119 mL) sour cream
> 1–2 teaspoons lemon juice
> 1 green onion, thinly sliced
> 2 teaspoons minced garlic
> 2–3 drops red pepper sauce
> Salt and cayenne pepper, to taste
> Dippers: assorted vegetables, bread sticks, or crackers

1. Process the artichoke hearts, cream cheese, Parmesan cheese, mayonnaise, sour cream, and lemon juice in food processor until smooth. Stir in the green onion, garlic, and red pepper sauce. Season to taste with salt and cayenne pepper.

2. Bake in a small casserole, uncovered, at 350°F (180°C) until lightly browned, 20 to 25 minutes. Serve warm with dippers.

CURRY DIP (LACTO-OVO)

Raw sweet potato slices and broccoli florets are particularly good with this dip. This recipe comes from 1,001 Low-Fat Vegetarian Recipes *by Sue Spitler.*

12 SERVINGS (ABOUT 2 TABLESPOONS EACH)

1½ cups (356 mL) reduced-fat mayonnaise
½ cup (119 mL) sour cream
¼ cup (25 g) thinly sliced green onions
1½–2 teaspoons prepared horseradish
1½–2 teaspoons curry powder
2–3 teaspoons sugar
2–4 teaspoons lemon juice
Salt and white pepper, to taste
Dippers: assorted vegetable relishes and pita chips

1. Mix the mayonnaise, sour cream, green onions, horseradish, curry powder, and sugar. Season to taste with lemon juice, salt, and white pepper. Refrigerate several hours for the flavors to blend. Serve with dippers.

CHEESE AND SPINACH STUFFED MUSHROOMS (LACTO) >

Perfect party fare, with good-for-you mushrooms and spinach! Garnish the serving platter with curly endive.

12 SERVINGS (3 EACH)

36 medium cremini or white mushrooms

½ cup (75 g) chopped onion

5 ounces (142 g) baby spinach, thinly sliced

1 package (3 ounces [85 g]) Neufchatel or cream cheese, room temperature

⅛ teaspoon ground nutmeg

Salt and pepper, to taste

1. Remove the stems from the mushrooms and chop finely. Sauté the mushroom stems and onion in a lightly greased small skillet until softened, about 5 minutes. Add the spinach and stir until wilted, 1 to 2 minutes. Cool; mix in the cream cheese and nutmeg; season to taste with salt and pepper.

2. Place the mushroom caps in a baking pan and fill with the cheese mixture. Bake, uncovered, at 425°F (220°C) until hot, 5 to 8 minutes.

VARIATION

Orzo Stuffed Mushrooms—Make the recipe as above, using 2 ounces (57 g) baby spinach, adding ¾ cup (120 g) cooked orzo and substituting ¾ teaspoon dried Italian seasoning for the nutmeg. Bake as above, loosely covered with foil.

SUN-DRIED TOMATO HUMMUS (LACTO)

Sun-dried tomatoes and herbs embellish this Mediterranean favorite.

8 SERVINGS (ABOUT ¼ CUP [59 ML] EACH)

1 can (15 ounces [426 g]) chickpeas (garbanzo beans), rinsed, drained

⅓ cup (79 mL) 2% plain yogurt

2–3 tablespoons (30–45 mL) tahini (sesame seed paste)

3 cloves garlic

4 sun-dried tomato halves (not packed in oil), finely chopped

1 teaspoon dried oregano

1 teaspoon mint leaves

2–3 teaspoons lemon juice

Salt and white pepper, to taste

Dippers: pita breads, cut into wedges

1. Process the chickpeas (garbanzo beans), yogurt, tahini, and garlic in a food processor until smooth. Stir in the sun-dried tomatoes, oregano, and mint; season to taste with the lemon juice, salt, and white pepper. Refrigerate 1 to 2 hours for the flavors to blend. Serve with dippers.

VARIATION

Parthenon Platter—Make the hummus as above and spoon it into a 6-inch (15-cm) flattened mound on a serving platter. Combine 4 chopped canned artichoke hearts, ½ cup (80 g) halved grape tomatoes, 6 sliced Greek olives, ⅓ cup (51 g) crumbled feta cheese, 2 tablespoons olive oil, and ¾ teaspoon Italian seasoning; toss and spoon over the hummus.

PINTO BEAN AND AVOCADO DIP (VEGAN)

Avocado and tomato brighten this well-flavored bean dip. Increase the amount of jalapeño pepper if you dare!

12 SERVINGS (ABOUT 2 TABLESPOONS EACH)

> 1 can (15 ounces [426 g]) pinto beans, rinsed, drained
> ¾ cup (113 g) finely chopped onion
> 2 cloves garlic
> ½ jalapeño pepper, minced
> 3 tablespoons (3 g) finely chopped cilantro
> 1 large tomato, chopped
> ½ medium avocado, peeled, pitted, chopped
> Salt and pepper, to taste
> Baked tortilla chips

1. Process the beans in a food processor or blender until smooth; add the onion, garlic, jalapeño pepper, and cilantro and process until blended. Mix in the tomato and avocado; season to taste with salt and pepper. Refrigerate 1 to 2 hours for the flavors to blend. Serve with tortilla chips.

CHUTNEY CHEESE SPREAD (LACTO)

Enjoy these flavors inspired by India. Ginger contributes heat as well as flavor to the spread, so adjust according to your taste.

8 SERVINGS (ABOUT 2 TABLESPOONS EACH)

1 package (8 ounces [227 g]) Neufchatel or cream cheese, softened

1 cup (4 ounces [114 g]) shredded Cheddar cheese

½ cup (119 mL) chopped mango chutney, divided

¼ cup (38 g) finely chopped onion

2 tablespoons raisins, chopped

1–2 teaspoons finely chopped gingerroot

1 clove garlic, minced

½–1 teaspoon curry powder

1–2 tablespoons chopped dry-roasted cashews

Thinly sliced green onion tops, for garnish

Pita chips or assorted vegetables

1. Mix the cheeses, 2 tablespoons chutney, onion, raisins, gingerroot, garlic, and curry powder until blended (do not beat, or the Neufchatel will become thin in texture). Refrigerate 1 to 2 hours for the flavors to blend.

2. Mound the spread on a plate; spoon remaining 6 tablespoons (90 mL) chutney over or around the spread. Sprinkle with the cashews and green onion tops; serve with pita chips or vegetables.

SOUPS AND GRAVIES

CREAM OF BROCCOLI SOUP (VEGAN)

A simple roux thickens this soup, and a hint of lemon sparkles up the flavor.

6 SERVINGS (2 CUPS [474 ML] EACH)

2 quarts (1.90 L) rice or soy beverage

2 or 3 heads fresh broccoli, cut into florets

¼ cup (59 mL) olive oil

⅓ cup (45 g) white spelt flour

3 shallots, peeled and very finely diced

Zest and juice of 1 lemon

2 teaspoons white pepper

½ teaspoon grated nutmeg

½ teaspoon cayenne pepper

Salt and freshly ground black pepper, to taste

1. Fill a large pot with water and heat to boiling.

2. Fill a large saucepan with the rice or soy beverage and place it over medium heat.

3. Salt the boiling water liberally. Add the broccoli florets and blanch about 8 minutes. Drain the florets in a colander and cool them under cold running water. Alternatively, place the florets in a microwave-safe bowl with a cup of water, cover, and microwave on high about 10 minutes.

4. In a large, heavy-bottomed soup pot, heat the olive oil over medium-high heat. Whisk in the flour just until it begins to darken, about 4 minutes.

5. Whisk in the shallots, lemon zest, white pepper, nutmeg, and cayenne pepper.

6. Cook the flour mixture 2 minutes. Add the hot soy beverage, 2 cups (474 mL) at a time, whisking between each addition smooth and creamy.

7. Add most of the broccoli, reserving 10 or 15 of the smallest florets to use for garnish.

8. Simmer about 15 minutes, and then blend the soup with an immersion blender or blend it in batches in a food processor, until smooth, returning it to the pot and heating it to serving temperature.

9. Add the reserved florets. Stir in the lemon juice and season to taste with salt. Serve in bowls garnished with a grinding of black pepper, if desired.

SUMMER GREENS SOUP WITH ROASTED SHALLOTS (VEGAN)

This bright green soup has a high vitamin and mineral content and tastes absolutely fabulous. Start by roasting the shallots. This recipe calls for spinach and two different varieties of kale, but you can substitute any greens.

8 SERVINGS (2 CUPS [474 ML] EACH)

> 6 whole shallots, peeled
> ½ cup (119 mL) plus 3 tablespoons (45 mL) olive oil, divided
> 2 quarts (1.90 L) good-quality vegetable stock
> 1 quart (948 mL) soy or rice beverage, heated
> 1 red onion, diced
> 1 teaspoon ground white pepper
> 1 teaspoon ground nutmeg
> 1 bunch green kale, stemmed and chopped
> 1 bunch lacinato kale, stemmed and chopped
> 1 bunch spinach, stemmed and chopped
> 2 cups (600 g) fresh or frozen green peas
> Salt, to taste
> Seasoned rice vinegar, to taste

1. Place the shallots in a small roasting pan with ½ cup (119 mL) olive oil and ½ cup (119 mL) water. Cover tightly with foil and roast at 400°F (200°C) 35 to 45 minutes, or until the shallots are very soft and slightly browned. Remove from the oven and set aside.

2. Heat the stock and soy beverage to boiling in a large saucepan over medium-high heat. Reduce the heat to a simmer.

3. In a large, heavy-bottomed soup pot, heat the remaining 3 tablespoons (45 mL) of olive oil over medium heat. Add the onion, white pepper, and nutmeg, and cook until the onion is transparent.

4. Add the greens and peas and stir well, cooking until the greens are wilted and begin to release their moisture.

5. Stir in the stock and soy beverage. Add the roasted shallots.

6. Blend with an immersion blender or transfer to a blender in batches. Return the soup to the pot, and heat to serving temperature. Season to taste with salt and seasoned rice vinegar. Serve immediately.

TORTELLINI SOUP WITH KALE (OVO)

Fast and easy to make when there's little time to cook!

8 SERVINGS (ABOUT 1½ CUPS [356 ML] EACH)

> 1 cup (100 g) sliced leek, or green onions
> 3 cloves garlic, minced
> 1 tablespoon olive oil
> 3 quarts (2.85 L) reduced-sodium vegetable broth
> 2 cups (12 ounces [341 g]) kale, coarsely chopped
> 1 cup (75 g) sliced mushrooms
> ½ package (9-ounce [255-g]) mushroom, or herb, tortellini
> Salt and white pepper, to taste

1. Sauté the leek and garlic in oil in a large saucepan until the leek is tender, 5 to 8 minutes.

2. Add the broth and heat to boiling; stir in the kale and mushrooms. Reduce heat and simmer, covered, 5 minutes.

3. Add the tortellini and simmer, uncovered, until al dente, about 7 minutes; season to taste with salt and white pepper.

SWEET POTATO CHIPOTLE CHILI (VEGAN) >

Chipotle peppers are dried, smoked jalapeño peppers. When canned, they are in adobo sauce, which is made with ground chilies and spices. The chipotle peppers add a distinctive smoky flavor to this robust dish; taste before adding a second pepper.

4 SERVINGS (1½ CUPS [356 ML] EACH)

1 cup (135 g) frozen stir-fry pepper blend

2 teaspoons minced gingerroot

1 teaspoon minced garlic

1 teaspoon cumin seeds

1 tablespoon peanut or canola oil

3 cups (500 g) cubed peeled sweet potatoes (½ inch [13 mm])

2 cans (15 ounces [426 g] each) black beans, rinsed, drained

1 can (14½ ounces [411 g]) chili-style chunky tomatoes, undrained

1–2 chipotle peppers in adobo sauce, chopped

1 cup (237 mL) water or vegetable broth

Salt, to taste

1. Sauté the stir-fry pepper blend, gingerroot, garlic, and cumin seeds in oil in a large saucepan until tender, about 5 minutes.

2. Add the remaining ingredients, except salt, and heat to boiling. Reduce heat and simmer, covered, until the sweet potatoes are tender, about 15 minutes. Season to taste with salt.

BLACK BEAN SOUP WITH SUN-DRIED TOMATOES AND CILANTRO CREAM (LACTO)

Cilantro Cream adds a fresh accent to this south-of-the-border favorite.

4 SERVINGS (ABOUT 1½ CUPS [356 ML])

1 cup (150 g) chopped onion

2 cloves garlic, minced

1 jalapeño chili, minced

3 cups (711 mL) vegetable stock

3 cups (516 g) cooked dried black beans, or 2 cans (15 ounces [426 g] each) black beans, rinsed, drained

¾ cup (41 g) sun-dried tomatoes (not in oil)

¾ teaspoon ground cumin, dried oregano leaves

¼–½ teaspoon hot pepper sauce

Salt and pepper, to taste

¼ cup (4 g) chopped cilantro

Cilantro Cream (recipe follows)

1. Sauté the onion, garlic, and jalapeño pepper in a lightly greased large saucepan until tender, 5 to 8 minutes. Add the stock, beans, sun-dried tomatoes, cumin, and oregano to the saucepan; heat to boiling. Reduce heat and simmer, covered, 10 minutes.

2. Process the soup in a food processor or blender until smooth. Season to taste with hot pepper sauce, salt, and pepper; stir in cilantro. Garnish each bowl of soup with dollops of Cilantro Cream.

CILANTRO CREAM

ABOUT ⅓ CUP (79 ML)

⅓ cup (79 mL) sour cream
2 tablespoons minced cilantro
1 teaspoon lemon or lime juice
¾ teaspoon ground coriander
2–3 dashes white pepper

1. Combine all the ingredients.

CINNAMON-SPICED PUMPKIN SOUP (LACTO)

For convenience, 2 cans (16 ounces [454 g] each) pumpkin can be substituted for the fresh pumpkin. Any yellow winter squash such as butternut, Hubbard, or acorn can also be used.

4 SERVINGS (ABOUT 1¼ CUPS [296 ML] EACH)

4 cups (464 g) cubed seeded peeled pumpkin
2 cups (474 mL) half-and-half or 2% milk
1–2 tablespoons light brown sugar
½ teaspoon ground cinnamon
¼–½ teaspoon ground nutmeg
Snipped chives, for garnish

1. Cook the pumpkin in a medium saucepan, covered, in 1 inch (2.5 cm) of simmering water until tender, about 15 minutes; drain.

2. Process the pumpkin and half-and-half in a food processor or blender; return to the saucepan. Stir in the brown sugar, cinnamon, and nutmeg and heat to boiling; reduce heat and simmer, uncovered, 5 minutes. Sprinkle each bowl of soup with chives.

VIDALIA ONION SOUP (VEGAN)

The mild sweetness of Vidalia onions makes this soup special, but try it with other flavorful onion varieties too. This recipe comes from 1,001 Low-Fat Vegetarian Recipes by Sue Spitler.

8 SERVINGS (ABOUT 1¼ CUPS [296 ML] EACH)

6 cups (1½ pounds [681 g]) thinly sliced Vidalia onions

2 cloves garlic, minced

1 teaspoon sugar

⅓ cup (40 g) all-purpose flour

6 cups (1.40 L) reduced-sodium vegetable broth

1½ teaspoons dried sage leaves

2 bay leaves

Salt, cayenne, and white pepper, to taste

Snipped chives, for garnish

1. Add the onions and garlic to a lightly greased saucepan and cook, covered, over medium-low heat until wilted, 8 to 10 minutes. Stir in sugar and continue cooking, uncovered, until the onions are lightly browned. Stir in the flour; cook about 1 minute longer. Add the broth, sage and bay leaves; heat to boiling. Reduce heat and simmer, covered, 30 minutes. Discard the bay leaves.

2. Process half the soup in a food processor or blender until smooth; return to the saucepan and season to taste with salt, cayenne pepper, and white pepper. Serve warm, or chilled; sprinkle each bowl of soup with chives.

CURRIED BUTTERNUT SQUASH SOUP (VEGAN)

Acorn or Hubbard squash can also be used in this fragrant soup.

8 SERVINGS (ABOUT 1 CUP [237 ML] EACH)

½ cup (109 g) chopped onion

1 clove garlic, mashed

2 teaspoons (10 mL) olive oil

4 cups (948 mL) reduced-sodium vegetable broth

2 pounds (908 g) butternut squash, peeled, seeded, cubed

2 medium tomatoes, chopped

1½ teaspoons curry powder

1 cup (16 g) coarsely chopped cilantro leaves and stems

Salt and pepper, to taste

Cilantro sprigs, for garnish

1. Sauté the onion and garlic in oil in a large saucepan until tender, about 5 minutes. Add the broth, squash, tomatoes, and curry powder and heat to boiling; reduce heat and simmer, covered, until the squash is tender, about 10 minutes.

2. Process the soup and cilantro in a blender or food processor until smooth; season to taste with salt and pepper. Serve warm; garnish each bowl of soup with cilantro sprigs.

VARIATION

Savory Herbed Squash Soup—Make the recipe above, omitting the tomatoes, curry powder, and cilantro; add ¾ teaspoon each dried thyme and marjoram leaves and ¼–½ teaspoon ground mace.

MUSHROOM GRAVY (VEGAN)

This is easy to make, and your friends and family will love you for it. This recipe comes from The Veganopolis Cookbook *by David Stowell and George Black.*

8 CUPS (1.90 L)

6 cups (1.40 L) vegetable stock
¼ cup (59 mL) olive or canola oil
½ cup (69 g) spelt flour or other flour
½ cup (75 g) finely diced shallots
1 tablespoon garlic powder
1 tablespoon onion powder
2 teaspoons ground white pepper
1 teaspoon ground black pepper
½ teaspoon cayenne pepper
1 cup (75 g) fresh button or cremini mushrooms, stemmed
   and quartered
2 tablespoons tamari

1. Heat the stock to boiling in a Dutch oven or soup pot.

2. In a second saucepan, heat the oil over medium heat. Add the flour and whisk to form a roux. Cook the roux about 3 minutes.

3. Add the shallots, garlic powder, onion powder, and white and black pepper, and cook 2 to 3 minutes. Add the mushrooms and cook 5 more minutes, stirring constantly.

4. Ladle about ¼ of the boiling stock into the mushroom mixture and stir until well blended. Blend in ⅓ of the remaining stock. Little by little, add the rest of the stock until the desired consistency is reached.

5. Stir in the tamari and serve.

SALADS

LENTIL SALAD WITH FETA CHEESE (LACTO)

There are lots of flavor, texture, and color contrasts in this salad.

6 SERVINGS (ABOUT 1⅓ CUPS [316 ML] EACH)

1¼ cups (240 g) dried brown lentils

2½ cups (593 mL) reduced-sodium vegetable broth

1½ cups (54 g) coarsely chopped iceberg lettuce

1½ cups (240 g) coarsely chopped tomatoes

½ cup (75 g) thinly sliced celery

½ cup (75 g) yellow bell pepper

½ cup (75 g) thinly sliced onion

½ cup (65 g) chopped cucumber

¾ cup (113 g) crumbled feta cheese

Balsamic Dressing (see recipe page 66)

Salt and pepper, to taste

1. Heat the lentils and broth to boiling in a large saucepan; reduce heat and simmer, covered, until the lentils are just tender, about 25 minutes. Drain; cool.

2. Combine the lentils, lettuce, tomatoes, celery, bell pepper, onion, cucumber, and cheese; drizzle the Balsamic Dressing over and toss. Season to taste with salt and pepper.

CREAMY POTATO SALAD (VEGAN)

The trick with potato salad is to cook the potatoes just to the point of tenderness. Over- and undercooking give equally unsatisfactory results. Take a potato chunk out of the water while you are cooking them and pierce it with a fork. The potatoes are done when the fork goes through with just a little pressure. At that point, drain the potatoes immediately and rinse them under cold running water. Or better still, drain them and plunge them into a large quantity of iced, salted water.

9 SERVINGS

> 3 pounds (1.36 kg) potatoes, peeled and cut into ½-inch (1-cm) cubes
> 2 tablespoons salt, plus more to taste
> 2 teaspoons white pepper
> 2 teaspoons dry mustard
> 1 cup (150 g) finely diced celery
> ¼ cup (38 g) finely diced red onion
> 4 scallions, thinly sliced
> 1 cup (237 mL) Mayo (see recipe page 68) or store-bought vegan mayonnaise

1. Place the potatoes in a large pot, and cover with cold water.

2. Add 2 tablespoons salt to the water, and heat to boiling. Simmer 8 minutes before beginning to check potatoes for doneness.

3. When the potatoes are fork tender, drain them in a colander and rinse under cold running water until cool. Alternatively, drain and plunge them into a large quantity of iced water, then drain again once cooled.

4. Transfer the potatoes to a large bowl. Season them with the white pepper and dry mustard.

5. Add the celery, onions, and scallions and mix gently. Add the Mayo and mix gently. Season to taste with salt.

ROASTED POTATO SALAD (VEGAN)

This recipe produces a fabulously flavored potato salad. The potatoes are roasted instead of boiled, and a simple vinaigrette replaces the mayonnaise. It is also a little lower in fat than a creamy potato salad.

6 SERVINGS

FOR THE SALAD:

4 large potatoes (about 2 pounds [908 g]), rinsed and cut into ½-inch (1-cm) pieces

2 teaspoons salt

2 teaspoons ground white pepper

¼ cup (59 mL) olive oil

⅓ cup (79 mL) apple cider vinegar

½ cup (15 g) finely chopped parsley

½ cup (75 g) finely diced celery

¼ cup (38 g) finely diced shallots

FOR THE VINAIGRETTE:

1 tablespoon Dijon mustard

1 teaspoon agave syrup

½ cup (119 mL) olive oil

2 tablespoons apple cider vinegar

1. Line a baking sheet with parchment paper.

2. Spread the potato pieces out on the baking sheet and pat dry. Season with the salt and white pepper. Drizzle with olive oil and, using your hands, toss the potato pieces until evenly coated with oil and seasonings.

3. Roast at 400°F (200°C) 35 to 45 minutes, or until the potatoes are lightly browned and fork tender. Remove from the oven and, while the potatoes are still warm, drizzle them with ⅓ cup apple cider vinegar. Let cool.

4. To make the vinaigrette, combine the Dijon mustard and agave syrup in a mixing bowl. Whisk in the olive oil until well blended. Add 2 tablespoons apple cider vinegar and whisk until blended.

5. Combine the roasted potatoes, parsley, celery, shallots, and vinaigrette in a large mixing bowl.

Note: To vary the flavor, add chopped fresh rosemary, thyme, and/or basil. Add finely sliced scallions and a few tablespoons of grainy mustard for a Bavarian-style potato salad. Try substituting roasted sweet potatoes for the regular potatoes. Or, best of all, use your imagination and invent your own combinations.

BRUSSELS SPROUTS AND PASTA SHELL SALAD (LACTO)

Make this colorful salad to celebrate the first summer harvest of Brussels sprouts.

4 SERVINGS (ABOUT 1½ CUPS [356 ML] EACH)

6 ounces (170 g) whole wheat pasta shells, cooked, cooled
2 cups (300 g) halved small Brussels sprouts, cooked, cooled
1 cup (160 g) chopped tomato
1 cup (150 g) sliced green bell pepper
¼ cup (38 g) thinly sliced red onion
Sun-Dried Tomato and Goat Cheese Dressing (see recipe page 67)
Salt and pepper, to taste
¼ cup (23 g) shredded Romano cheese

1. Toss the pasta, Brussels sprouts, tomato, bell pepper, onion, and Sun-Dried Tomato and Goat Cheese Dressing in a salad bowl; season to taste with salt and pepper. Sprinkle with the cheese.

BRUNCH TOFU SALAD (VEGAN) >

This salad makes a highly nourishing and delicious treat anytime. Use it on sandwiches or wraps, or serve it on toast as a starter.

3 CUPS (711 ML)

1 pound (454 g) firm tofu, drained, rinsed, and cut into ¼-inch (6-mm) dice

1 cup (150 g) finely diced celery

¼ cup (8 g) finely chopped fresh parsley

¼ cup (38 g) very finely diced shallots

¼ cup (38 g) finely diced red or orange bell peppers

2 teaspoons ground turmeric

1 teaspoon ground white pepper

2 teaspoons onion powder

1 clove garlic, minced, or 1 teaspoon garlic powder

½ teaspoon salt, to taste

1 pinch cayenne pepper or a few red pepper flakes

1 cup (237 mL) Mayo (see recipe page 68) or store-bought vegan mayonnaise

1. Combine the tofu, celery, parsley, shallots, and bell pepper in a large bowl.

2. Add the turmeric, white pepper, garlic, and salt to the Mayo and stir well until blended. Add the seasoned Mayo to the tofu mixture and stir to blend. Season to taste with salt.

3. Serve as a sandwich or as a salad. This salad also works well in a wrap with romaine or spinach. It will keep, if covered and refrigerated, for 3 days or longer.

Note: Add rinsed capers, Kalamata olives, or diced pickles for flavor and visual appeal.

FARMER CRANBERRY WALNUT SALAD (VEGAN)

This recipe is a delicious variation on cranberry sauce for a holiday meal. This recipe comes from The Veganopolis Cookbook *by David Stowell and George Black.*

4 SERVINGS (½ CUP [119 ML] EACH)

1 (14-ounce [397-g]) can vegan jellied cranberries

½ cup (57 g) chopped toasted walnuts

½ cup (75 g) finely diced celery

1 tablespoon agave syrup or turbinado sugar

1 teaspoon salt (optional)

2 tablespoons orange juice

1 tablespoon orange zest

1. Combine all the ingredients in a bowl. Taste for seasoning and adjust as needed.

2. Serve chilled.

VARIATION

Cranberry Holiday Mold Salad—Soak 2 tablespoons agar powder or flakes in a blend of ¼ cup (59 mL) orange juice and 2 tablespoons water. Heat the mixture to a boil. Reduce the heat and simmer for 5 minutes. Add to the salad. Stir well, pour into the mold, and chill for a few hours before serving. At serving time, invert the mold on a chilled plate and garnish with whole cranberries and orange peel.

Note: Add chopped apples, blueberries, or firm pears if desired.

GRILLED TOFU SALAD WITH AVOCADO (VEGAN)

This salad recipe produces a nice combination of texture and color.

1 SERVING

> ⅓ pound (152 g) extra-firm tofu, marinated in your favorite marinade
>
> Generous handful mesclun lettuce mix
>
> 2 tablespoons seasoned rice vinegar
>
> 1 fresh avocado, peeled, pitted, quartered, and sliced lengthwise
>
> 1 fresh tomato, sliced
>
> 1 cucumber, stripe peeled and sliced
>
> Finely chopped parsley, for garnish

1. Preheat the grill or broiler.

2. Grill the tofu on each side until it is fully cooked and firm. Slice it lengthwise in half and grill the newly cut sides. Remove from the grill and slice it into triangles.

3. Dress a handful of mesclun with the seasoned rice vinegar or dressing of your choice, and mound it in the center of a chilled plate. Arrange ¼ of a sliced avocado and a few slices of tomato and cucumber on one side of the plate.

4. Top the salad with the grilled tofu triangles. Garnish with finely diced parsley and serve.

BLACK-EYED BETTY SALAD (VEGAN) >

This colorful salad features a robust pesto and offers high nutritional value. It may also be heated and served atop a plate of sautéed greens or mashed potatoes. Served cold, this salad is a popular item on our lunch menu.

6 SERVINGS

> 1 cup (237 mL) Basil Pesto (see recipe page 70)
> 1 (15-ounce [426-g]) can black-eyed peas, rinsed, drained
> ½ cup (118 mL) finely diced red bell pepper
> ½ cup (118 mL) finely diced yellow bell pepper
> ¼ cup (38 g) finely diced red onion
> ¼ teaspoon nutmeg

1. Place the black-eyed peas in a saucepan. Add water to cover by 1 inch (2.5 cm) and bring to a simmer.

2. Simmer 10 minutes, then drain and rinse well under cold running water until cool.

3. Transfer the peas to a bowl and stir in the pesto.

4. Fold in the red and yellow bell pepper, onion and nutmeg.

5. Taste the salad for seasoning and adjust as necessary.

Note: Serve over a bed of fresh spinach. Garnish with croutons. This salad also makes a nice wrap filling.

BLACK BEAN AND SMOKED TOFU SALAD (VEGAN)

The smoky flavor of the tofu is a pleasant contrast to the picante chili, fresh cilantro, and Mustard-Honey Dressing. Purchased smoked tofu can be used. This recipe comes from 1,001 Low-Fat Vegetarian Recipes by Sue Spitler.

4 SERVINGS (ABOUT 1¼ CUPS [296 ML] EACH)

> 2 cans (15 ounces [426 g] each) black beans, rinsed, drained
>
> Mesquite-Smoked Tofu (recipe follows), cubed
>
> 1 cup (160 g) chopped tomato
>
> 1 cup (150 g) chopped red bell pepper
>
> ½ cup (75 g) sliced red onion
>
> ¼ cup (4 g) finely chopped cilantro
>
> ¼ cup (8 g) finely chopped parsley
>
> 2 teaspoons finely chopped jalapeño chili
>
> 2 teaspoons roasted garlic
>
> Mustard-Honey Dressing (see recipe page 67)

1. Combine all the ingredients in a salad bowl and toss.

MESQUITE-SMOKED TOFU

4 SIDE-DISH SERVINGS

2 packages (10½ ounces [298 g] each) light firm tofu, halved lengthwise

1. Arrange hot charcoal around edges of grill and place a shallow pan of water in center. Sprinkle hot coals with mesquite chips that have been soaked in water and well drained. Place tofu on greased rack. Smoke, covered, 20 to 30 minutes, or longer for a more intense smoky flavor.

Note: For range-top smoking, sprinkle 2 to 3 tablespoons mesquite smoking bits (very small mesquite chips, available in canisters at hardware and home improvement stores and some supermarkets) or mesquite shavings in bottom of Dutch oven; place wire rack in Dutch oven. Place tofu on greased pan on rack; heat, covered, over high heat 5 minutes. Lift lid just enough to make sure pan is filled with smoke; reduce heat to medium-low and cook, covered, 20 to 30 minutes.

DRESSINGS, CONDIMENTS, AND SAUCES

CAESAR DRESSING (VEGAN)

This recipe produces a classic, creamy Caesar dressing. Olive oil, garlic, lemon juice, and red wine vinegar are essential.

4 CUPS (948 ML)

8 ounces (227 g) firm tofu, drained and rinsed

8 ounces (227 g) soft tofu, drained and rinsed

⅓ cup (79 mL) freshly squeezed lemon juice

⅓ cup (79 mL) red wine vinegar

1 tablespoon vegan Worcestershire sauce*

1 tablespoon freshly ground black pepper

4 cloves garlic, peeled and crushed

1 cup (237 mL) extra virgin olive oil or more as needed

Salt, to taste

1. Process the tofu in a food processor or a large blender until smooth. With the machine running, add the remaining ingredients, except salt, adding enough olive oil for the desired consistency. (Caesar dressing should be creamy but not overly thick, so it will nicely coat lettuce.) Season to taste with salt.

Available in many areas. If you can't find it, use 1 tablespoon tamari and 1 tablespoon balsamic vinegar.

RANCH DRESSING (VEGAN)

Scallions and chopped parsley enhance this vegan version of the American standard.

2 CUPS (474 ML)

8 ounces (227 g) firm tofu, rinsed, drained
8 ounces (224 g) soft tofu, rinsed, drained
Juice of 1 lemon
2 teaspoons (10 mL) agave syrup
1 cup (100 g) sliced scallions
½ cup (15 g) finely chopped parsley
2 tablespoons seasoned rice vinegar
2 teaspoons ground white pepper
1½ cups (356 mL) grapeseed or canola oil
¼ cup (59 mL) water
Salt, to taste

1. Process the soft and firm tofu in a food processor until very smooth.

2. Add the lemon juice, agave syrup, scallions, parsley, vinegar, and white pepper, and process again until well mixed.

3. With the machine running, add the oil in a thin stream until it is completely incorporated. The dressing should be shiny and smooth.

4. Season to taste with salt. Ranch dressing should be thick enough to nicely coat the lettuce—thinner than a mayonnaise, but thicker than a vinaigrette. You may add water to adjust the density.

THOUSAND ISLAND DRESSING (VEGAN)

It is, after all, comparatively vulgar in relation to rémoulades, aiolis, and other elegant dressings, but there is really something appealing about Thousand Island Dressing.

3¹⁄₃ CUPS (790 G)

>   2 cups (474 mL) Mayo (see recipe page 68)
>   1 cup (237 mL) ketchup
>   ¹⁄₃ cup (79 mL) dill pickle relish

1.   Combine all the ingredients and blend well.

BALSAMIC DRESSING (VEGAN)

ABOUT 1¹⁄₃ CUP (79 ML)

>   3 tablespoons (45 mL) balsamic or red wine vinegar
>   2 tablespoons olive oil
>   2 tablespoons lemon juice
>   2 cloves garlic, minced
>   ½ teaspoon dried thyme leaves

1.   Mix all the ingredients.

MUSTARD–HONEY DRESSING (VEGAN)

ABOUT ½ CUP (119 ML)

3–4 tablespoons (45–60 mL) olive oil
3–4 tablespoons (45–60 mL) cider vinegar
1 tablespoon Dijon mustard
1–2 tablespoons honey
½ teaspoon dried oregano leaves
1–2 dashes red pepper sauce

1. Mix all the ingredients.

SUN-DRIED TOMATO AND GOAT CHEESE DRESSING (VEGAN)

ABOUT ½ CUP (119 ML)

3 sun-dried tomato halves (not in oil), softened, finely
  chopped
1 tablespoon olive oil
2 tablespoons white wine vinegar
2 tablespoons lemon juice
2–3 tablespoons (30–45 mL) goat cheese
2 cloves garlic, minced
½ teaspoon dried marjoram leaves

1. Mix all the ingredients.

MAYO (VEGAN)

One nice thing about making your own mayonnaise is that you can season it just to your taste. It's also very economical.

3 CUPS (711 ML)

8 ounces (227 g) firm tofu, drained and rinsed
8 ounces (227 g) soft tofu, drained and rinsed
¼ cup (59 mL) apple cider vinegar
2 teaspoons agave syrup
1 tablespoon fresh lemon juice
½ teaspoon dry mustard
2 teaspoons ground white pepper
1 cup (237 mL) grapeseed or canola oil
Salt, to taste

1. Process the firm and soft tofu together in a blender or food processor until smooth.

2. Add the vinegar, agave syrup, lemon juice, mustard, and white pepper and blend again.

3. While the machine is running, add the oil in a thin stream until it is incorporated. If the mayonnaise is too thick at this point, you may add a little water.

4. Season to taste with salt and perhaps a little more fresh lemon juice.

TROPICAL SALSA (VEGAN)

A fruit and vegetable salsa with a cool, refreshing flavor!

6 SERVINGS (ABOUT ¼ CUP [59 ML] EACH)

½ cup (83 g) cubed pineapple

½ cup (70 g) cubed papaya

½ cup (83 g) cubed mango

½ cup (80 g) cubed tomato

¼ cup (43 g) rinsed drained canned black beans

¼ cup (33 g) chopped seeded cucumber

½ teaspoon minced jalapeño pepper

2 tablespoons finely chopped cilantro

¼ cup (59 mL) orange juice

1 tablespoon lime juice

2–3 teaspoons sugar

1. Combine all the ingredients in a bowl and toss.

BASIL PESTO (VEGAN)

Rice vinegar is sold in two varieties: plain and seasoned. The seasoned variety is what makes sushi rice taste the way it does. Its sweet/salty/acid flavor is unique among vinegars and adds just the right touch to this pesto, which is great for pastas, pizzas, and sandwiches.

2 CUPS (474 ML)

8 cloves garlic, peeled and minced

2 bunches fresh basil, stemmed (about 3 cups [72 g])

2 ounces (57 g) pine nuts

¼ cup (59 mL) seasoned rice vinegar

3 tablespoons (45 mL) red wine vinegar

1½ cups (356 mL) extra-virgin olive oil, or more as needed

Salt, to taste

1. Process the garlic, basil leaves, pine nuts, and vinegars in a food processor until smooth.

2. With the machine still running, add the olive oil in a thin stream until the pesto coats a spoon thickly.

3. Season to taste with salt.

Notes: This pesto will keep, if covered and refrigerated, for at least a week. If you place it in sterile, sealed jars, it will keep even longer. If the top of the pesto oxidizes over time, simply spoon the very top layer off and discard. The remainder should be fine. For a little variety, add ½ cup (119 mL) soaked and drained sun-dried tomatoes.

ALFREDO SAUCE (LACTO)

Serve this favorite Parmesan-flavored sauce over traditional fettuccine noodles.

4 SERVINGS (ABOUT ½ CUP [119 ML] EACH)

3 tablespoons (42 g) butter or margarine

¼ cup (30 g) all-purpose flour

2½ cups (593 mL) 2% or skim milk

¼ cup (23 g) grated Parmesan cheese

⅛ teaspoon ground nutmeg

½ teaspoon salt

¼ teaspoon black pepper

1. Melt butter in medium saucepan; add flour and cook, stirring 1 minute. Whisk in milk; heat to boiling. Boil, whisking, until thickened, about 1 minute. Reduce heat to low and whisk in remaining ingredients; cook 1 to 2 minutes longer.

BÉCHAMEL SAUCE (VEGAN)

This sauce can be substituted for any savory white sauce. You can add crushed garlic for a delicious creamy garlic sauce or melt shredded vegan cheese into it and use it as a vegan Mornay sauce. This recipe comes from The Veganopolis Cookbook *by David Stowell and George Black.*

2 QUARTS (1.90 L)

> 2 quarts (1.90 L) soy or rice beverage
> ⅓ cup (79 mL) olive oil
> ⅔ cup (92 g) white spelt flour or other white flour
> 4 shallots, peeled and very finely diced
> 2 teaspoons ground white pepper
> 2 teaspoons ground nutmeg
> Salt, to taste

1. Heat the soy beverage to boiling in a large saucepan over medium-high heat, then reduce the heat to a simmer.

2. Heat the olive oil in a large, heavy-bottomed saucepan over medium-high heat. Whisk in the flour to form a roux.

3. Add the shallots, white pepper, and nutmeg and cook, whisking constantly, for about 5 minutes or until the roux is fragrant and just beginning to darken.

4. Add the hot soy beverage in 1-cup (237-mL) batches, whisking to blend after each addition. Continue adding and whisking until all the liquid is incorporated. Season to taste with salt.

Notes: To augment the flavor of the Béchamel, try studding a small, whole, peeled onion with whole cloves and placing it in the finished sauce. Cook the sauce over very low heat for an additional 30 minutes, stirring occasionally. Remove and discard the onion. You may also try adding a few bay leaves when you add the onion, removing them before using the sauce. This recipe makes a large quantity for a full pan casserole. We suggest making this large batch and freezing the unused portion.

PIZZA SAUCE (VEGAN)

A simple sauce that can also be used on burgers, loaves, or other en-
trées. This recipe comes from 1,001 Low-Fat Vegetarian Recipes *by*
Sue Spitler.

4 SERVINGS (¼ CUP EACH [59 ML])

> ¼ cup (38 g) chopped onion
> ¼ cup (38 g) green bell pepper
> 2 cloves garlic, minced
> 1 can (8 ounces [240 mL]) reduced-sodium tomato sauce
> ½ teaspoon dried basil leaves
> ½ teaspoon dried oregano leaves
> Salt and black pepper, to taste

1. Sauté onion, bell pepper, and garlic in lightly greased medium saucepan until tender, about 5 minutes. Stir in tomato sauce, basil, and oregano; heat to boiling. Reduce heat and simmer, uncovered, until sauce thickens, about 5 minutes. Season to taste with salt and black pepper.

MARINARA SAUCE (VEGAN)

We always use diced tomatoes rather than crushed tomatoes, whole tomatoes, or tomato sauce because they cook down into an appealing, chunky sauce you can serve as is or blend smooth.

6 CUPS (1.4 L)

½ cup (119 mL) extra-virgin olive oil

1 large red onion, finely diced

4 cloves garlic, crushed

1 tablespoon Italian seasoning blend

1 teaspoon freshly ground black pepper

1 small pinch red pepper flakes

1 (32-ounce [960 mL]) can diced tomatoes or an equivalent amount diced, fresh tomatoes

Salt, to taste

1. Heat the oil in a large saucepan over medium heat.

2. Add the onion, garlic, Italian seasoning, pepper, and pepper flakes. Cook until the onion is softened. Add the diced tomatoes and stir well.

3. Simmer at least 40 minutes, and season to taste with salt.

Note: You can spike the sauce at the end with a splash of balsamic vinegar or fresh chopped basil, if desired.

ROASTED TOMATO–HERB SAUCE (VEGAN)

ABOUT 3 CUPS (711 ML)

2½ pounds (1.14 kg) Italian plum tomatoes, halved

1 leek (white part only), cut into ¾-inch (2-cm) pieces

1 medium onion, cut into wedges

2 medium carrots, cut into ¾-inch (2-cm) pieces

2 cloves garlic, peeled

Vegetable oil cooking spray

½ teaspoon dried oregano leaves

½ teaspoon dried marjoram leaves

½ cup (15 g) loosely packed basil leaves

Salt and pepper, to taste

1. Arrange the vegetables in a single layer on a greased foil-lined jelly-roll pan; spray with cooking spray and sprinkle with the oregano and marjoram. Roast at 425°F (220°C) on top oven rack until the vegetables are browned and tender, about 40 minutes.

2. Process the vegetables and basil in a food processor or blender until almost smooth. Season to taste with salt and pepper.

ENCHILADA SAUCE (VEGAN)

Many Mexican sauces are a simple combination of puréed ingredients that are then cooked or "fried" until thickened to desired consistency.

8 SERVINGS (ABOUT ¼ CUP [59 ML] EACH)

> 1 ancho chili, seeds and veins discarded
> 2 medium tomatoes, chopped
> ⅓ cup (50 g) chopped red bell pepper
> ⅓ cup (50 g) chopped onion
> 2 cloves garlic, minced
> ½ teaspoon dried marjoram leaves
> ⅛ teaspoon ground allspice
> 1 bay leaf
> Salt, to taste

1. Cover the ancho chili with boiling water in a small bowl; let stand until softened, 10 to 15 minutes. Drain. Process the chili, and remaining ingredients, except bay leaf and salt, in a food processor or blender until almost smooth. Cook the sauce and bay leaf in a lightly greased small skillet over medium heat until thickened to a medium consistency; about 5 minutes. Discard bay leaf; season to taste with salt.

POBLANO CHILI SAUCE (VEGAN)

Fast and easy to make, this sauce will vary in hotness depending upon the individual poblano chili and the amount of chili powder used.

8 SERVINGS (ABOUT ¼ CUP [59 ML] EACH)

2 medium tomatoes, chopped

½ medium poblano chili, seeds and veins discarded, chopped

1 small onion, chopped

2 cloves garlic, minced

1–2 tablespoons chili powder

Salt and pepper, to taste

1. Cook all the ingredients, except the salt and pepper, in a lightly greased large skillet until the poblano chili and onion are very tender, 8 to 10 minutes. Process in a food processor or blender until smooth; season to taste with salt and pepper.

ENTRÉES

TACOS PICADILLO (VEGAN)

This Mexican favorite is seasoned with raisins, almonds, sweet spices, and jalapeño pepper.

6 ENTRÉE SERVINGS (1 TACO EACH)

¼ cup (38 g) chopped onion

2 cloves garlic, minced

½ small jalapeño pepper, minced

1 teaspoon canola oil

¾ package (12-ounce [341-g] size) vegetarian ground beef

½ cup (80 g) chopped tomato

¼ cup (41 g) dark raisins

¼ cup (27 g) toasted slivered almonds

1–2 teaspoons cider vinegar

1 teaspoon ground cinnamon

¼ teaspoon dried oregano leaves

¼ teaspoon ground cloves

¼ teaspoon ground allspice

Salt and pepper, to taste

6 low-carb whole wheat tortillas, warm

Tomato Poblano Salsa (recipe follows)

1. Sauté the onion, garlic, and jalapeño pepper in oil in a medium skillet until tender, about 5 minutes. Add the remaining ingredients, except the salt, pepper, tortillas, and Tomato Poblano Salsa. Cook over medium heat until mixture is hot, about 5 minutes; season to taste with salt and pepper. Spoon about ⅓ cup mixture onto each tortilla and roll up. Serve with Tomato Poblano Salsa.

TOMATO POBLANO SALSA

ABOUT 1 CUP (237 ML)

¾ cup (120 g) chopped tomato

¼ cup (38 g) chopped poblano chili

¼ cup (4 g) cilantro

2 tablespoons finely chopped onion

1 teaspoon finely chopped jalapeño pepper

1 clove garlic, minced

Salt, to taste

1. Mix all the ingredients, except salt; season to taste with salt.

CRANBERRY CHEESE MELT (LACTO)

Lots of melted cheese, with cranberry and walnut accents. This recipe comes from 1,001 Low-Fat Vegetarian Recipes *by Sue Spitler.*

4 ENTRÉE SERVINGS

¼ package (8-ounce [227-g] size) Neufchatel or cream cheese, room temperature

¼ cup (28 g) shredded Swiss cheese

¼ cup (29 g) chopped walnuts

8 slices whole wheat bread

½ medium onion, thinly sliced

¼ cup (59 mL) whole-berry cranberry sauce

½ cup (57 g) shredded Cheddar cheese

Vegetable cooking spray

1. Mix the cream cheese, Swiss cheese and walnuts; spread on 4 slices bread. Top with the onion slices, cranberry sauce, Cheddar cheese, and remaining bread. Spray both sides of the sandwiches lightly with cooking spray; cook the sandwiches in a large skillet over medium heat until browned, 3 to 5 minutes on each side.

SHELLS STUFFED WITH SPINACH AND TOFU (LACTO) >

Firm tofu substitutes for the usual ricotta cheese in this delicious dish.

4 ENTRÉE SERVINGS (5 SHELLS EACH)

> 1½ cups (225 g) chopped onions
> 6 cloves garlic, minced
> 1 package (10 ounces [284 g]) baby spinach
> ¾ cup (23 g) finely chopped parsley
> 1½ teaspoons dried basil leaves
> ½ package (14-ounce [397-g] size) firm tofu, finely chopped
> 1½ cups (170 g) shredded mozzarella cheese
> 2 tablespoons grated Parmesan cheese
> 20 jumbo pasta shells (6 ounces [170 g]), cooked, warm
> 2 cups (237 mL) Marinara Sauce (see recipe page 74)

1. Sauté the onions and garlic in a lightly greased skillet until transparent, 3 to 5 minutes. Add the spinach, parsley and basil and cook, covered, over medium heat until the spinach is wilted, 3 to 5 minutes. Remove from heat and cool slightly; stir in the tofu and cheeses.

2. Stuff each shell with about 3 tablespoons cheese mixture. Arrange the shells in a baking pan and spoon the Marinara Sauce over. Bake at 350°F (180°C), loosely covered, until hot, 20 to 25 minutes.

Note: Begin cooking the pasta shells before preparing the rest of the recipe.

CURRIED SWEET POTATO COUSCOUS (VEGAN)

Versatile couscous blends easily with a variety of vegetable flavors.

4 ENTRÉE SERVINGS

¼ cup (38 g) sliced onion

2 cloves garlic, minced

1–2 tablespoons olive oil

2 medium sweet potatoes, cooked, diced

1–1½ teaspoons curry powder

¼ cup (41 g) raisins

¼ cup (29 g) walnuts

1 cup (237 mL) reduced-sodium vegetable broth

⅔ cup (120 g) uncooked couscous

1 cup (65 g) thinly sliced kale

Salt and pepper, to taste

1. Sauté the onion and garlic in olive oil in a large saucepan until tender, 2 to 3 minutes. Add the sweet potatoes; cook until lightly browned, about 5 minutes. Stir in the curry powder, raisins, walnuts, and broth; heat to boiling.

2. Add the couscous and kale, stirring with a fork; remove from the heat and let stand, covered, until the couscous is tender and broth is absorbed, about 5 minutes. Season to taste with salt and pepper. Transfer to a serving bowl.

SPAGHETTI SQUASH WITH ROASTED TOMATO–HERB SAUCE AND ARTICHOKES (LACTO)

The squash can also be grilled. Wrap squash halves in foil and grill over medium-hot coals until tender, 30 to 40 minutes, turning occasionally.

4 ENTRÉE SERVINGS

> 1 small spaghetti squash, halved, seeded
> 1 package (9 ounces [255 g]) frozen artichoke hearts,
>   thawed, halved
> Roasted Tomato-Herb Sauce (see recipe page 75)
> ¼ cup (23 g) grated Parmesan cheese

1. Place the squash halves, cut sides down, in a roasting pan and add 1 inch (2.5 cm) hot water. Bake, covered, on the bottom oven rack at 400°F (200°C) until tender, about 45 minutes.

2. Using fork, scrape the squash to separate into strands, leaving squash in shells to serve.

3. Stir the artichoke hearts into the Roasted Tomato-Herb Sauce and cook over medium heat until hot, about 5 minutes; spoon into the squash halves. Sprinkle with the cheese and toss.

ASIAN FRIED RICE (OVO)

The combination of wild and white rice adds a new dimension to an Asian favorite. Lightly scrambled egg is a traditional addition to many fried rice recipes; it can be omitted, if desired.

4 ENTRÉE SERVINGS (ABOUT 1½ CUPS [356 ML] EACH)

> 2 cups (300 g) broccoli florets and sliced stalks
>
> 1 cup (150 g) halved snow peas
>
> ¾ cup (78 g) bean sprouts
>
> ¾ cup (96 g) sliced carrots
>
> ¾ cup (56 g) sliced shiitake mushrooms
>
> ¾ cup (113 g) chopped celery
>
> ¾ cup (113 g) green bell pepper
>
> 1 teaspoon minced garlic
>
> 1 teaspoon finely chopped gingerroot
>
> ½ cup (119 mL) reduced-sodium vegetable broth
>
> 2 tablespoons reduced-sodium soy sauce
>
> 1½ cups (240 g) cooked white rice
>
> 1½ cups (285 g) wild rice
>
> 1 egg, lightly scrambled, crumbled
>
> Salt and pepper, to taste

1. Stir-fry the vegetables, garlic, and gingerroot in a lightly greased large wok or skillet until crisp-tender, 5 to 8 minutes. Add the broth and soy sauce; stir in the rice, wild rice, and scrambled egg and stir-fry 2 to 3 minutes longer. Season to taste with salt and pepper.

PORCINI RISOTTO (LACTO)

Use dried shiitake or Chinese black mushrooms if you can't find porcini.

1 cup (237 mL) boiling water
¼–½ ounce (7–14 g) dried porcini mushrooms
1 small onion, chopped
3 cloves garlic, minced
1 small tomato, seeded, chopped
1 teaspoon dried sage leaves
1½ cups (285 g) uncooked arborio rice
1½ quarts (1.4 mL) reduced-sodium vegetable broth
¼ cup (23 g) grated Parmesan cheese
Salt and pepper, to taste
2 tablespoons toasted pine nuts
2 tablespoons finely chopped fresh sage

1. Pour boiling water over the mushrooms in a bowl; let stand until the mushrooms are soft, about 15 minutes; drain, reserving liquid. Slice the mushrooms, discarding the tough stems.

2. Sauté the mushrooms, onion, and garlic in a lightly greased large saucepan until tender, about 5 minutes. Stir in the tomato and dried sage; cook 2 minutes longer. Stir in the rice and cook over medium heat until the rice begins to brown, 2 to 3 minutes, stirring frequently.

3. Heat the broth and reserved porcini liquid to boiling in a medium saucepan; reduce heat to medium-low to keep broth hot. Add the broth to the rice mixture, ½ cup (119 mL) at a time, stirring constantly over medium heat until the broth is absorbed before adding another ½ cup (119 mL). Continue the process until the rice is al dente and the mixture is creamy, 20 to 25 minutes; stir in the cheese. Season to taste with salt and pepper; sprinkle with the pine nuts and fresh sage.

EGGPLANT PROVENÇAL (LACTO)

This dish can be assembled several hours in advance; sprinkle with the breadcrumb mixture just before baking.

4 ENTRÉE SERVINGS (1½ CUPS [356 ML] EACH)

2 pounds (908 g) eggplant, peeled, cubed (¾ inch [18 mm])
2 medium green bell peppers, sliced
4 cups (640 g) chopped tomatoes
1 cup (150 g) chopped onion
1 clove garlic, minced
¼ cup (45 g) sliced black or pimiento-stuffed olives
1 tablespoon drained capers
½–¾ teaspoon dried basil leaves
½–¾ teaspoon dried oregano leaves
Salt and pepper, to taste
1½ cups (170 g) shredded mozzarella cheese

1. Sauté the eggplant, bell peppers, tomatoes, onion, and garlic in a lightly greased large skillet 3 to 4 minutes; cook, covered, over medium heat, until the vegetables are tender, 8 to 10 minutes, stirring occasionally. Stir in the olives, capers, basil and oregano; season to taste with salt and pepper.

2. Spoon the eggplant mixture into an 11 x 7-inch (27.5 x 17.5-cm) baking dish; sprinkle with the cheese. Bake, uncovered, at 350°F (180°C), until bubbly and browned, about 30 minutes.

JUST PEACHY BEAN POT (VEGAN)

Peaches, peach nectar, dried fruit, and mango chutney add special flavor to this bean combo.

6 ENTRÉE SERVINGS (ABOUT 1⅓ CUPS [316 ML] EACH)

> 1 cup (150 g) chopped onion
> 1 clove garlic, minced
> 1–1½ teaspoons curry powder
> ½ teaspoon ground allspice
> ½ teaspoon red pepper flakes
> 1 tablespoon margarine
> 1 can (15 ounces [426 g]) navy beans, rinsed, drained
> 2 cans (15 ounces [426 g] each) red kidney beans, rinsed, drained
> 1½ cups (225 g) diced peaches
> ½ cup (56 g) coarsely chopped mixed dried fruit
> ½ cup (119 mL) mango chutney
> ½–¾ cup (119–178 mL) peach nectar
> 2 tablespoons cider vinegar
> Salt and pepper, to taste

1. Sauté the onion, garlic, curry powder, allspice, and red pepper flakes in margarine in a small skillet until tender, about 5 minutes. Mix with the remaining ingredients, except salt and pepper, in a 2½-quart (2.4-L) casserole; season to taste with salt and pepper. Bake, covered, at 350°F (180°C) 30 minutes; if thicker consistency is desired, bake, uncovered, about 15 minutes more.

FALAFEL PITAS WITH TAHINI DRESSING (LACTO) >

The falafel mixture can also be shaped into meatballs, coated lightly with unseasoned dry bread crumbs, sprayed with cooking spray and baked at 375°F until browned, about 15 minutes. Serve in pitas.

4 ENTRÉE SERVINGS

1½ cups (164 g) cooked dried, or drained canned, chickpeas (garbanzo beans), coarsely puréed
¼ cup (8 g) finely chopped parsley
2 tablespoons chopped onion
2 cloves garlic, minced
1–2 tablespoons lemon juice
¼ cup (30 g) all-purpose flour
1¼ teaspoons ground cumin
Salt and pepper, to taste
2 pita breads, halved
Tahini Dressing (recipe follows)
¼ cup (40 g) chopped tomato
¼ cup (40 g) chopped thinly sliced green onions
¼ cup (33 g) chopped cucumber

1. Mix the garbanzo beans, parsley, onion, garlic, lemon juice, flour, and cumin in a bowl; season to taste with salt and pepper.

2. Shape the falafel mixture into 4 burgers and cook in a lightly greased skillet until browned, 3 to 4 minutes on each side. Arrange the falafel burgers in the pitas; drizzle 2 tablespoons of the Tahini Dressing over each falafel burger. Spoon the combined tomato, cucumber, and sliced green onions into the pitas.

TAHINI DRESSING

ABOUT 1⅓ CUPS (316 ML)

> ⅓ cup (79 mL) 2% plain yogurt
> 2–3 tablespoons (30–45 mL) tahini (sesame seed paste)
> 1 small clove garlic, minced
> ½–1 teaspoon lemon juice

1. Mix all the ingredients; refrigerate until ready to use.

Note: Make the Tahini Dressing before preparing the rest of the recipe.

EGGPLANT PARMESAN SANDWICHES (LACTO-OVO)

Try crumbled feta cheese as a delicious substitute for the mozzarella.

4 ENTRÉE SERVINGS

> 4 thick slices eggplant (scant ¾ inch [2.5 cm])
> 1 egg, beaten
> ⅓ cup (50 g) seasoned dry bread crumbs
> 2 tablespoons grated Parmesan cheese
> 4 ounces (114 g) sliced mozzarella cheese
> 4 French rolls, or hoagie buns, toasted
> 2 roasted small red peppers, halved
> Pizza Sauce (see recipe page 73)

1. Dip the eggplant slices in the egg and coat them with the combined bread crumbs and Parmesan cheese. Cook in a lightly greased large skillet over medium heat until tender and browned, about 5 minutes on each side. Top each eggplant slice with 1 ounce cheese; cook, covered, until cheese is melted, 2 to 3 minutes. Serve in buns with roasted red peppers and Pizza Sauce.

Note: Make the Pizza Sauce before preparing the rest of the recipe.

ORECCHIETTE WITH ARTICHOKE HEARTS, MUSHROOMS, AND PEPPERS (LACTO)

Other pasta shapes, such as cappelletti (little hats), farfalle (bow ties), or rotini (corkscrews), can be substituted.

4 ENTRÉE SERVINGS

> 4 ounces (114 g) shiitake or cremini mushrooms, sliced
> 1 coarsely chopped red bell pepper
> 1 coarsely chopped yellow bell pepper
> 4 cloves garlic, minced
> 2 teaspoons olive or canola oil
> ½ can (15-ounce [426-g] size) quartered artichoke hearts, rinsed, drained
> Salt and pepper, to taste
> 3 cups (12 ounces [341 g]) orecchiette, cooked, warm
> ¼ cup (38 g) crumbled feta cheese
> 2 tablespoons (15 g) coarsely chopped walnuts

1. Sauté the mushrooms, bell peppers, and garlic in oil in a large skillet until tender, 3 to 5 minutes. Add the artichoke hearts and cook until hot, 3 to 4 minutes. Season to taste with salt and pepper. Toss with the pasta; sprinkle with the feta cheese and walnuts.

Note: Begin cooking the orecchiette before preparing the rest of the recipe.

BLACK BEAN MEATBALLS (LACTO)

Nicely picante and spiced, these meatballs will be loved by all!

6 ENTRÉE SERVINGS (5 EACH)

2 cans (15 ounces [426 g] each) black beans, rinsed, drained

1 medium jalapeño pepper, chopped

2 teaspoons finely chopped gingerroot

1 cup (16 g) loosely packed cilantro leaves

¼ cup (23 g) flaked unsweetened coconut

½ teaspoon curry powder

Salt and pepper, to taste

4 cups (628 g) cooked kasha, cracked wheat, or couscous, warm

Cucumber Yogurt (recipe follows)

1. Process the beans, jalapeño pepper, gingerroot, cilantro, coconut, and curry powder in a food processor until smooth. Season to taste with salt and pepper.

2. Shape the bean mixture into 30 balls and place in a baking pan. Bake at 350°F (180°C) until hot, 15 to 20 minutes. Serve on the kasha; spoon the Cucumber Yogurt over.

Note: Begin cooking the kasha and make the Cucumber Yogurt before preparing the rest of the recipe.

CUCUMBER YOGURT

ABOUT 2 CUPS (474 ML)

1 cup (237 mL) 2% plain yogurt

1 cup (130 g) seeded, finely chopped cucumber

1 teaspoon dried dill weed

1. Combine all the ingredients.

BOURBON STREET RED BEANS AND RICE (VEGAN)

The New Orleans favorite, at its best!

4 ENTRÉE SERVINGS (ABOUT 1¼ CUPS [296 ML] EACH)

1 cup (184 g) dried red beans
2–3 cups (474–711 mL) reduced-sodium vegetable broth
1 cup (150 g) chopped onion
1 cup (150 g) chopped green bell peppers
1 cup (150 g) chopped celery
½–1 jalapeño pepper, finely chopped
1 teaspoon dried thyme leaves
1 teaspoon dried oregano leaves
½ teaspoon dried sage leaves
½ teaspoon ground cumin
2 bay leaves
¼ teaspoon red pepper sauce
¼ teaspoon cayenne pepper
4–6 drops liquid smoke
Salt, to taste
4 cups (640 g) cooked rice, warm

1. Cover the beans with 2 inches (5 cm) of water in a large saucepan; heat to boiling and boil 2 minutes. Remove from the heat and let stand 1 hour; drain and return to the saucepan.

2. Add 2 cups of the broth to the beans and heat to boiling; simmer, covered, 30 minutes. Add the onion, bell peppers, celery, jalapeño pepper, thyme, oregano, sage, cumin, and bay leaves; simmer, covered, until beans are tender, 30 to 45 minutes, adding more broth if necessary (the beans should be moist but without excess liquid). Discard the bay leaves.

3. Stir in the red pepper sauce, cayenne pepper, and liquid smoke; season to taste with salt. Serve over rice.

SIDE DISHES

ARDENNES-STYLE SCALLOPED POTATOES (VEGAN)

The Ardennes region of France is up north, near the Belgian border. It is where you will find Charleville, the birthplace of poet Arthur Rimbaud. This recipe comes from The Veganopolis Cookbook *by David Stowell and George Black.*

8 SERVINGS

> 6 large potatoes, peeled, sliced ⅛ inch (3 mm) thick, and placed in cold water to cover
> 1 recipe Béchamel Sauce (see recipe page 72)
> Salt and pepper
> 12 juniper berries, crushed
> 4 tablespoons (8 g) finely chopped fresh rosemary
> 1 Spanish onion, peeled and sliced thinly

1. Oil a baking dish.

2. Drain the potato slices and transfer them to a large pot of salted water. Bring the pot to a boil, lower the heat to a simmer, and cover the pot. Let simmer for about 8 minutes or until the potatoes are flexible but still firm. Drain and rinse them in a large colander.

3. Pour the Béchamel Sauce into the baking dish and spread it evenly over the bottom. Arrange a layer of potato slices on top of the sauce. Season the potato slices with salt, pepper, and a pinch of the crushed juniper berries and chopped rosemary. Then arrange a layer of sliced onion over the top. Top with sauce. Continue building the layers this way until you have filled the dish. Finish with the sauce and a generous amount of black pepper.

4. Bake until golden brown, about 45 minutes. Serve immediately.

VEGGIE-STUFFED BAKERS (LACTO)

The potatoes are greased and baked for a crispy skin; for a softer skin, wrap in foil.

6 SERVINGS

2 large Idaho potatoes (8–10 ounces each)
⅓ cup (79 mL) sour cream or 2% plain yogurt
¾ cup (85 g) shredded Cheddar cheese, divided
1 cup (150 g) chopped onion
1 cup (150 g) chopped green bell pepper
½ cup (80 g) whole-kernel corn
4 cloves garlic, minced
Salt and pepper, to taste
1 cup (150 g) broccoli florets, cooked crisp-tender

1. Pierce the potatoes with a fork; grease lightly and bake at 400°F (200°C) until tender, about 1 hour. Cut the potatoes lengthwise into halves; let stand until cool enough to handle.

2. Scoop out the potatoes, being careful to leave the shells intact. Mash the potatoes in a medium bowl, adding the sour cream and half the Cheddar cheese.

3. Sauté the onion, bell pepper, corn, and garlic in a lightly greased medium skillet until tender, about 5 minutes. Mix into the potato mixture; season to taste with salt and pepper.

4. Spoon the potato mixture into the shells; arrange the broccoli on top and sprinkle with the remaining cheese. Bake, uncovered, at 350°F (180°C) until hot, 20 to 30 minutes.

ASPARAGUS WITH PEANUT SAUCE (VEGAN)

Asian flavors are the perfect complement to spring's freshest asparagus. The asparagus can be served warm or chilled.

6 SERVINGS

> 2 tablespoons peanut butter
> ¼ cup (50 g) sugar
> 2–3 tablespoons (30–45 mL) reduced-sodium tamari soy sauce
> 3–4 teaspoons rice wine (sake), dry sherry, or water
> 1 teaspoon grated gingerroot
> 1½ pounds (681 g) asparagus spears, cooked crisp-tender

1. Mix the peanut butter, sugar, soy sauce, rice wine, and gingerroot until smooth. Serve with the asparagus.

POLENTA (VEGAN)

This basic recipe can be modified to your taste—note the variations below. This recipe comes from 1,001 Low-Fat Vegetarian Recipes *by Sue Spitler.*

6 SIDE-DISH SERVINGS (ABOUT ½ CUP [119 ML] EACH)

> **3 cups (711 mL) water**
> **¾ cup (120 g) yellow cornmeal**
> **Salt and pepper, to taste**

1. Heat the water to boiling in a medium saucepan; gradually stir in the cornmeal. Cook over medium to medium-low heat, stirring constantly, until the polenta thickens enough to hold its shape but is still soft, 5 to 8 minutes. Season to taste with salt and pepper.

VARIATIONS

Blue Cheese Polenta (Lacto)—Stir ½ cup (75 g) crumbled blue cheese, or other blue veined cheese, into the cooked polenta.

Goat Cheese Polenta (Lacto)—Stir ¼ to ½ cup (38–75 g) crumbled goat cheese into the cooked polenta.

Garlic Polenta (Vegan)—Sauté ¼ cup (38 g) finely chopped onion and 4 to 6 cloves minced garlic in 1 tablespoon olive oil; add water, as above, and complete the recipe.

GRILL-ROASTED VEGETABLES WITH POLENTA (VEGAN)

The vegetables can also be oven-roasted at 425°F (220°C) for 30 to 40 minutes. Polenta can be made 2 to 3 days in advance.

4 ENTRÉE SERVINGS (ABOUT 1½ CUPS [356 ML] EACH)

4 medium tomatoes

4 medium red onions

2 medium red bell peppers

2 medium yellow summer squash

2 medium eggplant, unpeeled, cut in ½-inch (13-mm) rounds

1 large bulb garlic, top trimmed

2 tablespoons balsamic or red wine vinegar

1 tablespoon olive oil

1 teaspoon lemon juice

½ teaspoon dried rosemary leaves

½ teaspoon dried sage leaves

½ teaspoon dried thyme leaves

Polenta (see recipe page 101)

4 slices Italian bread, toasted

1. Cut the tomatoes and red onions into wedges; cut the bell peppers and squash into 1-inch slices. Grill the vegetables and garlic on a greased rack over medium-hot coals, turning occasionally, until browned and tender, about 30 minutes. Combine the vegetables, except the garlic, in a bowl; toss with the combined vinegar, oil, lemon juice, rosemary, sage, and thyme.

2. Cut the polenta into 8 wedges; cook in a lightly greased large skillet until browned on both sides. Overlap 2 polenta wedges on each serving plate; spoon the vegetables over. Serve the roasted garlic to spread on bread.

APPLE–PECAN ACORN SQUASH (VEGAN)

Fruit and maple flavors complement sweet, baked winter squash.

4 SERVINGS

1 large acorn squash, quartered, seeded
½ cup (56 g) coarsely chopped mixed dried fruit
1 small sweet apple, cored, coarsely chopped
¼–½ cup (27–55 g) coarsely chopped, toasted pecans
½ teaspoon ground cinnamon
⅛ teaspoon ground nutmeg
⅛ teaspoon mace
¼–½ cup (59–119 mL) maple syrup

1. Place the squash quarters, cut sides up, in a baking pan; add ½-inch (13 mm) hot water. Bake, covered, at 400°F (200°C) until the squash is fork-tender, about 30 minutes.

2. Spoon the combined dried fruit, apple, pecans, cinnamon, nutmeg, and mace into squash; drizzle with the maple syrup. Bake, loosely covered, at 350°F (180°C) until apples are tender, about 10 minutes.

CREAMED SPINACH (LACTO) >

Try this recipe with other healthful greens, such as Swiss chard or kale.

4 SERVINGS

2 packages (10 ounces [284 g] each) spinach, stems trimmed
¼ cup (38 g) finely chopped onion
2 teaspoons butter or margarine
2 tablespoons all-purpose flour
1 cup (237 mL) 2% milk or half-and-half
¼ cup (59 mL) sour cream
Ground nutmeg, to taste
Salt and pepper, to taste

1. Rinse the spinach and place in a large saucepan; cook, covered, over medium-high heat until wilted, 3 to 4 minutes; drain.

2. Sauté the onion in butter in a small saucepan until tender, 3 to 5 minutes. Stir in the flour; cook 1 minute, stirring. Whisk in the milk; heat to boiling. Boil, whisking, until thickened, about 1 minute. Remove from the heat and stir in the sour cream. Pour the sauce over the spinach and mix lightly; season to taste with nutmeg, salt, and pepper.

VARIATION

Spinach au Gratin—Prepare the recipe as directed above, reserving ¼ cup (59 mL) sauce; mix the spinach and remaining sauce and spoon into a small casserole. Spread reserved ¼ cup (59 mL) sauce over spinach; sprinkle with ¼ cup (23 g) grated Parmesan or Cheddar cheese. Bake, uncovered, at 375°F (190°C) until cheese is melted, 5 to 8 minutes.

SPAGHETTI SQUASH PARMESAN (LACTO)

The delicate flavor of the squash is complemented by the combination of Italian seasoning and Parmesan cheese.

4 SERVINGS

1 spaghetti squash (2½–3 pounds [1.14–1.40 kg]), cut lengthwise into halves, seeded

2 tablespoons sliced green onions

1 teaspoon minced garlic

1–2 tablespoons butter or margarine

¼ cup (59 mL) reduced-sodium vegetable broth

1 teaspoon dried Italian seasoning

½ cup Parmesan cheese

Salt and pepper, to taste

1. Place the squash, cut sides down, in a baking pan; add ½ inch [13 mm] hot water. Bake, covered, at 400°F (200°C) until fork tender, 30 to 40 minutes. Fluff the strands of squash with the tines of a fork, leaving the squash in the shells.

2. Sauté the green onions and garlic in butter in a small saucepan until tender, 3 to 4 minutes. Stir in the broth and Italian seasoning; heat to boiling. Spoon half the mixture into each squash half and toss; sprinkle with the Parmesan cheese and toss. Season to taste with salt and pepper.

GREENS-STUFFED BAKED TOMATOES (LACTO)

We've used turnip greens, but any other flavorful greens, such as kale, mustard greens, or spinach, may be substituted.

6 SERVINGS

> 6 medium tomatoes
> 10 ounces fresh or frozen turnip greens, cooked, coarsely chopped
> ½ teaspoon dried chervil leaves
> ½ teaspoon dried marjoram leaves
> Salt and pepper, to taste
> 1 tablespoon grated Parmesan cheese
> 1 tablespoon unseasoned dry bread crumbs

1. Cut a thin slice from the top of each tomato; scoop pulp from tomatoes, discarding seeds. Chop the pulp and mix with the turnip greens, chervil, and marjoram; season to taste with salt and pepper.

2. Spoon the mixture into the tomatoes and sprinkle with the combined cheese and bread crumbs. Place the tomatoes in a baking pan and bake at 350°F until tender, about 20 minutes.

SPICY RICE (LACTO)

This aromatic spiced dish of East Indian origins will complement many meals. The turmeric lends a beautiful yellow color to the rice.

1 medium onion, sliced
1 clove garlic, minced
1 tablespoon olive oil
1 cup (190 g) uncooked basmati rice
½ cup (119 mL) 2% plain yogurt
1–2 cardamom pods, crushed
¼ teaspoon ground turmeric
¼ teaspoon ginger
⅛ teaspoon red pepper flakes
2 cups (474 mL) reduced-sodium vegetable broth
Salt and pepper, to taste
1 small tomato, cut into 8 wedges
1 tablespoon finely chopped cilantro

1. Sauté the onion and garlic in oil in a large saucepan until tender, about 8 minutes. Stir in the rice; cook over medium heat until the rice begins to brown, about 5 minutes, stirring frequently.

2. Stir in the yogurt, cardamom, turmeric, ginger, and red pepper flakes; cook over medium-high heat 5 minutes, stirring frequently.

3. Add the broth and heat to boiling; reduce heat and simmer, covered, until the rice is tender, about 25 minutes. Season to taste with salt and pepper.

4. Place in serving bowl and garnish with the tomato wedges; sprinkle with the cilantro.

ORANGE CILANTRO RICE (VEGAN)

A perfect accompaniment to grilled or roasted tofu, tempeh, or vegetables.

> ½ cup (50 g) sliced green onions
> 1 cup (190 g) uncooked long-grain rice
> Grated zest of 1 small orange
> 2¼ cups (593 mL) water
> 2 tablespoons finely chopped cilantro
> Salt and pepper, to taste

1. Sauté the green onions in a lightly greased medium saucepan until tender, 3 to 5 minutes. Add the rice and orange zest; cook over medium heat until the rice is lightly browned, 2 to 3 minutes. Add the water and heat to boiling; reduce heat and simmer, covered, until the rice is tender, 20 to 25 minutes. Stir in the cilantro; season to taste with salt and pepper.

BREADS AND SAVORY BAKED GOODS

PEASANT BREAD (VEGAN)

Five grains and ground pecans combine in this hearty dense-textured country-style bread. Wonderful toasted, this bread is also delicious with honey.

2 SMALL LOAVES (8–10 SERVINGS EACH)

2 packages active dry yeast

½ cup warm water (110–115°F [50°C])

1¼ cups (170 g) whole wheat flour

½ cup (100 g) millet

½ cup (68 g) cracked wheat

½ cup (80 g) yellow cornmeal

½ cup (68 g) bulgur wheat

½ cup (45 g) quick-cooking oats

½ cup (55 g) ground pecans

1 teaspoon salt

1¼ cups (296 mL) lukewarm water

¼ cup (50 mL) honey

2 tablespoons canola oil

1–2 cups (121–242 g) unbleached all-purpose flour

1. Mix the yeast and ½ cup (119 mL) warm water in a large bowl; let stand 5 minutes. Mix in the remaining ingredients, except all-purpose flour; mix in enough all-purpose flour to make a smooth dough.

2.   Knead the dough on a floured surface until smooth and elastic, about 5 minutes (the dough will be heavy and difficult to maneuver). Place in a greased bowl; let rise, covered, in a warm place until doubled in size, about 1½ hours. Punch the dough down.

3.   Preheat the oven to 350°F (180°C). Grease a baking sheet.

4.   Divide the dough into halves; shape into round loaves on prepared baking sheet. Let stand, loosely covered, until doubled in size, about 1½ hours. Bake until the loaves are deep golden brown and sound hollow when tapped, about 40 minutes. Transfer to wire racks to cool.

CRANBERRY–NUT WHEAT LOAF (LACTO-OVO)

Dried cranberries and walnuts make this bread a perfect fall and winter offering. This recipe comes from 1,001 Low-Fat Vegetarian Recipes *by Sue Spitler.*

1 LOAF (16 SERVINGS)

> 1 package active dry yeast
>
> ¾ cup warm water (110–115°F [43–46°C])
>
> 3 tablespoons (45 mL) honey
>
> 2–3 tablespoons butter or margarine, room temperature
>
> 1 egg
>
> 1–2 cups (121–242 g) all-purpose flour, divided
>
> 1 cup (135 g) whole wheat flour
>
> 1 teaspoon salt
>
> 1 cup (112 g) dried cranberries
>
> ⅔ cup (76 g) coarsely chopped walnuts
>
> 2% or skim milk, for brushing

1. Mix the yeast, warm water, and honey in a large bowl; let stand 5 minutes. Add the butter, egg, 1 cup all-purpose flour, whole wheat flour, and salt, mixing until blended. Mix in cranberries, walnuts, and enough of the remaining 1 cup (121 g) all-purpose flour to make a smooth dough.

2.   Knead the dough on a floured surface until smooth and elastic, about 5 minutes. Place in a greased bowl; let rise, covered, in a warm place until doubled in size, 1 to 1½ hours. Punch the dough down.

3.   Shape the dough into a loaf and place in a greased 9 x 5-inch (22.5 x 12.5-cm) loaf pan. Let stand, covered, until doubled in size, about 45 minutes.

4.   Preheat the oven to 375°F (190°C).

5.   Brush the top of the loaf with milk. Bake until the loaf is golden and sounds hollow when tapped, 35 to 40 minutes. Remove from the pan and cool on a wire rack.

ROASTED RED PEPPER BREAD (LACTO-OVO)

Bake this loaf in a freeform long or round shape, or in a pan. For convenience, use jarred roasted red pepper.

1 LOAF (16 SERVINGS)

- 2¼–2¾ cups (272 g–333 g) all-purpose flour, divided
- ¾ cup (101 g) whole wheat flour
- ¼ cup (23 g) grated Parmesan cheese
- 1½ teaspoons dried Italian seasoning, divided
- ½ teaspoon salt
- 1 package fast-rising active dry yeast
- 1¼ cups (295 mL) very hot water (125–130°F [52–54°C])
- 1 tablespoon olive oil
- 4 ounces (112 g) mozzarella cheese, cubed (½ inch [1 cm])
- ½ cup (75 g) coarsely chopped roasted red pepper
- 1 egg white, beaten

1. Combine 2¼ cups (272 g) all-purpose flour, whole wheat flour, Parmesan cheese, 1 teaspoon Italian seasoning, salt, and yeast in a large bowl; add hot water and oil, mixing until blended. Mix in the mozzarella cheese, red pepper, and enough remaining ½ cup (61 g) all-purpose flour to make a smooth dough.

2. Knead the dough on a floured surface until smooth and elastic, about 5 minutes. Place in a greased bowl; let rise, covered, in a warm place until doubled in size, about 30 minutes. Punch dough down.

3. Shape the dough into a loaf and place in greased 9 × 5-inch (22.5 cm × 13-cm) loaf pan. Let stand, covered, until doubled in size, about 30 minutes.

4. Preheat oven to 375°F (190°C).

5. Make 3 or 4 slits in top of the loaf with a sharp knife. Brush egg white over dough and sprinkle with the remaining Italian seasoning. Bake until the loaf is golden and sounds hollow when tapped, 35 to 40 minutes. Remove from pan and cool on wire rack.

SWEET POTATO BRAIDS (LACTO-OVO) >

Canned pumpkin can be substituted for the sweet potatoes, if desired. For a variation, add ½ cup (83 g) raisins and/or ½ cup (57 g) coarsely chopped walnuts or pecans to the bread dough.

2 LOAVES (12 SERVINGS EACH)

> 2 packages active dry yeast
> ¼ cup warm 2% or skim milk (110–115°F [43–46°C])
> 1 cup (245 g) mashed cooked sweet potatoes
> 1¾ cups (315 mL) 2% or skim milk
> ¼ cup (59 mL) canola oil
> 1 egg
> 3–4 cups (363–484 g) all-purpose flour, divided
> 2 cups (270 g) whole wheat flour
> 1 teaspoon salt

1. Mix the yeast and warm milk in a large bowl; let stand 5 minutes. Mix in sweet potatoes, 1¾ cups (415 mL) milk, oil, and egg until blended; mix in 3 cups (363 g) all-purpose flour, whole wheat flour, and salt. Mix in enough of the remaining 1 cup (121 g) all-purpose flour to make a smooth dough.

2. Knead the dough on a floured surface until smooth and elastic, about 5 minutes. Place in a greased bowl; let rise, covered, in a warm place until doubled in size, about 1 hour. Punch the dough down.

3. Divide the dough into halves; divide each half into thirds. Roll pieces of dough into strips, 12 inches (30 cm) long. Braid 3 strips, folding ends under, and place on a greased cookie sheet. Repeat with the remaining dough. Let rise, loosely covered, until doubled in size, 30 to 45 minutes.

4. Preheat the oven to 375°F (190°C).

5. Bake until the breads are golden and sound hollow when tapped, 45 to 55 minutes. Transfer to wire racks to cool.

SPELT ENGLISH MUFFINS (VEGAN)

These are so good that you may want to bake enough for a whole week. They keep nicely in the refrigerator and can be sliced and toasted for breakfast. Leftover muffins make great garlic bread rounds or croutons. This recipe comes from The Veganopolis Cookbook *by David Stowell and George Black.*

8–10 MUFFINS

2½ teaspoons active dry yeast
2 teaspoons plus 1 pinch turbinado sugar
1 cup (237 mL) warm (110°F [43°C]) water
6 cups (810 g) unbleached white spelt flour, divided
1½ teaspoons salt
1 teaspoon ground white pepper
1 cup (237 mL) soy or rice beverage
1 teaspoon apple cider vinegar or fresh lemon juice
¼ cup (59 mL) vegan shortening, melted

1. Combine the yeast, a pinch of the turbinado sugar, and the warm water in a cup or small bowl and let stand until foamy for at least 10 minutes.

2. Combine 3 cups (711 mL) of the flour, salt, and white pepper in a large bowl.

3. Heat the soy beverage in a saucepan until just warm and add the remaining 2 teaspoons sugar and the apple cider vinegar.

4. Combine the shortening, soy beverage mixture, yeast mixture, and spelt flour mixture in a large bowl. Beat until smooth, then add the remaining 3 cups (711 mL) flour gradually, mixing thoroughly after each addition.

5. With your hands, work the dough in the bowl until all the ingredients are thoroughly blended. Transfer the dough to a floured surface and knead for 10 minutes.

6. Form the dough into a ball, place it in a lightly oiled bowl, and cover. Let it rise until doubled in size, about 45 minutes to 1 hour.

7. Punch the dough down and then roll it out on a floured surface into a rectangle about ½ inch (1 cm) thick. Cut out circles about 6 to 8 inches (15 to 20 cm) in diameter (a 3-inch [7.5-cm] diameter can with both ends cut out works well for cutting the circles) and place the circles on a nonstick surface (such as a baking sheet) in a warm place. Let rise again for about 45 minutes.

8. Preheat the oven to 250°F (120°C). Line a baking sheet with parchment paper.

9. Heat a large, heavy skillet (cast iron works best here) over medium-low and lightly oil it with about 2 teaspoons canola oil. Brown the muffins a few at a time, flipping them once until they are just browned, then transfer them to the prepared baking sheet.

10. Bake the muffins for about 30 minutes. Remove them from the oven and serve, or let them cool completely and store them in the refrigerator or freezer for later use. To toast them, simply slice horizontally in half beforehand.

ENGLISH MUFFIN BREAD (LACTO)

This quick and easy single-rise bread has a coarse texture similar to English muffins. It's delicious warm from the oven, or toasted, with honey.

1 LOAF (16 SERVINGS)

1½–2½ cups (182–303 g) all-purpose flour, divided
½ cup (45 g) quick-cooking oats
1 package active dry yeast
¼ teaspoon baking soda
1 teaspoon salt
1¼ cups (296 mL) warm 2% or skim milk (110–115°F
  [43–46°C])
1 tablespoon honey
Cornmeal, for coating

1. Combine 1½ cups (182 g) flour, oats, yeast, baking soda, and salt in large bowl. Add the milk and honey, mixing until smooth. Stir in enough of remaining 1 cup (121 g) flour to make a thick batter. Pour into a greased, cornmeal-coated 8 x 4-inch (21.25 x 11.25 cm) loaf pan. Let rise, covered, in a warm place until doubled in size, 45 to 60 minutes.

2. Preheat the oven to 400°F (200°C).

3. Bake until the bread is golden and sounds hollow when tapped, 25 to 30 minutes. Remove from the pan and cool on a wire rack.

VARIATION

Raisin Bread—Make the recipe as above, adding 1 teaspoon ground cinnamon and ½ cup (83 g) raisins to the batter; do not coat the loaf pan with cornmeal.

SQUASH DINNER ROLLS (LACTO-OVO)

Use pumpkin, Hubbard, or acorn squash for these rolls; mashed sweet potatoes can be used also. If a loaf is preferred, bake in a greased 8 × 4-inch (20 × 10-cm) loaf pan until the loaf is browned and sounds hollow when tapped, about 40 minutes.

24 ROLLS (1 EACH)

1½–2½ cups (182–303 g) all-purpose flour, divided

1 cup (135 g) whole wheat flour

2 packages fast-rising yeast

1–2 teaspoons salt

½ cup (119 mL) 2% or skim milk

¼ cup (59 mL) honey

1–2 tablespoons butter or margarine

¾ cup (184 g) mashed cooked winter squash

1 egg

1. Combine 1½ cups (182 g) all-purpose flour, whole wheat flour, yeast, and salt in large bowl. Heat the milk, honey, and butter in a small saucepan to 125–130°F (52–54°C); add to the flour mixture, mixing until smooth. Mix in the squash, egg, and enough of the remaining 1 cup (121 g) all-purpose flour to make a smooth dough.

2. Knead the dough on a floured surface until smooth and elastic, about 5 minutes. Place in a greased bowl; let stand, covered, in a warm place until doubled in size, 30 to 45 minutes. Punch dough down.

3. Preheat oven to 375°F (190°C). Grease muffin pans (24 cups).

4. Divide the dough into 24 pieces; shape into round rolls and place in muffin cups or on an unlined baking sheet. Bake until browned, 20 to 25 minutes.

VARIATION

Raisin-Walnut Pumpkin Bread—Make recipe as above, substituting mashed cooked or canned pumpkin for the squash and adding ½ cup each raisins (83 g) and chopped walnuts (57 g). Shape into a loaf in 9 × 5-inch (22.5 × 13-cm) loaf pan and let rise; bake at 375°F (190°C) until the loaf is browned and sounds hollow when tapped, about 40 minutes.

GREEN CHILI CORN BREAD (LACTO-OVO)

Corn bread, Southwest-style! If using mild canned chilies, consider adding a teaspoon or so of minced jalapeño pepper for a piquant accent.

9 SERVINGS

¼ cup (38 g) chopped red bell pepper

2 cloves garlic, minced

½ teaspoon cumin seeds, crushed

1¼ cups (200 g) yellow cornmeal

¾ cup (91 g) all-purpose flour

2 teaspoons baking powder

1 teaspoon sugar

½ teaspoon baking soda

½ teaspoon salt

1¼ cups (296 mL) buttermilk

½ cup (128 g) canned cream-style corn

1 can (4 ounces [114 g]) chopped hot, or mild, green chili peppers, well drained

2 eggs

3½ tablespoons (49 g) butter or margarine, melted

1. Sauté the bell pepper, garlic, and cumin seeds in a lightly greased small skillet until the pepper is tender, 2 to 3 minutes.

2. Preheat the oven to 425°F (220°C). Grease an 8-inch (20-cm) square baking pan.

3. Combine the cornmeal, flour, baking powder, sugar, baking soda, and salt in a large bowl. Mix in the bell pepper mixture, buttermilk, corn and chili peppers; spread in the prepared pan. Bake until golden, about 30 minutes. Cool in the pan on a wire rack; serve warm.

QUICK SELF-RISING BISCUITS (LACTO) >

Two cups all-purpose flour combined with 1 tablespoon baking powder and ½ teaspoon salt can be substituted for the self-rising flour.

18 BISCUITS

1 tablespoon vegetable shortening
2 cups (242 g) self-rising flour
¾–1 cup (178–237 mL) 2% or skim milk
1 tablespoon butter or margarine, melted

1. Preheat the oven to 425°F (220°C). Grease a 13 x 9-inch (32.5 x 22.5-cm) baking pan; brush with melted butter.

2. Cut the shortening into the flour in a medium bowl until the mixture resembles coarse crumbs. Stir in enough milk to make a soft dough. Roll the dough out on floured surface to ½-inch (13-mm) thickness; cut into 18 biscuits with 2-inch (5-cm) cutter. Place in the prepared pan.

3. Bake until golden brown, about 15 minutes.

VARIATIONS

Chive Biscuits—Make the biscuits as above, mixing 3 tablespoons (6 g) snipped fresh or dried chives into the dough.

Parmesan Biscuits—Make the biscuits as above; sprinkle with 2 tablespoons grated Parmesan cheese before baking.

QUEENLY QUINOA CRACKERS (VEGAN)

These crackers are gluten-free and very tasty.

ABOUT 30 CRACKERS

> 1½ cups (203 g) unbleached white spelt flour
> ½ cup (85 g) quinoa flour
> ½ teaspoon baking soda
> 1 teaspoon baking powder
> 1 teaspoon onion or garlic powder, or a mix of the two
> ½ teaspoon salt, plus more for sprinkling
> ½ teaspoon white pepper
> ¼ cup (59 mL) canola or safflower oil
> ⅓ cup (79 mL) plus 1 tablespoon water

1. Preheat the oven to 350°F (180°C). Line a baking sheet with parchment paper. Lightly oil the paper.

2. Combine all the dry ingredients in a medium bowl.

3. In a separate bowl, combine the water and oil. Slowly add the water mixture to the flour ingredients. Work the dough with your hands until the dough forms a ball.

4. On a floured surface or lightly oiled parchment paper, roll out the dough into a rectangle about ⅛ inch (3 mm) thick.

5. Cut the dough into a 30-square grid and place the squares on the prepared baking sheet. Pierce each square with the tines of a fork a few times and lightly salt them.

6. Bake for about 12 minutes and then flip the crackers over. Bake for an additional 2 or 3 minutes. Remove the pan from the oven and let cool.

7. Store in an airtight container.

DESSERTS

PEANUT BUTTER COOKIES (VEGAN)

This recipe comes from The Veganopolis Cookbook *by David Stowell and George Black.*

12 LARGE OR 18 SMALL COOKIES

> 3 cups (405 g) unbleached white spelt flour
> 1½ teaspoons baking powder
> ½ teaspoon baking soda
> 1 teaspoon salt
> 1 teaspoon ground cinnamon or allspice
> 1 cup (258 g) creamy peanut butter
> ½ cup (112 g) margarine, softened
> ¼ cup (59 mL) maple or agave syrup
> 1 tablespoon arrowroot powder
> 2 teaspoons vanilla extract
> 2 tablespoons warm water

1. Preheat the oven to 350°F (180°C). Line two baking sheets with parchment paper and lightly oil the paper.

2. Mix the flour, baking powder, baking soda, salt, and cinnamon in a large bowl.

3. In a separate bowl, combine the peanut butter, margarine, maple syrup, arrowroot, vanilla, and warm water. Stir until creamy and smooth.

4. Using a hand mixer, slowly blend the flour mixture into the peanut butter mixture. If the dough does not come together properly, use a little canola or safflower oil and work the dough with your hands.

5. Using a spoon or a 3-ounce (90-mL) ice cream scoop, drop scoops of the cookie dough on the prepared baking sheets. Imprint the tops with a fork for a classic style.

6. Bake 15 to 18 minutes. Remove from the oven and let cool for 30 minutes before removing them from the sheets and transferring them to a cooling rack. Store in a tightly covered container in a cool place.

CHOCOLATE CHIP COOKIES (LACTO-OVO)

America's favorite cookie! This recipe comes from 1,001 Low-Fat Vegetarian Recipes *by Sue Spitler.*

5 DOZEN COOKIES

> 8 tablespoons (112 g) butter or margarine, room temperature
> 1 cup (225 g) packed light brown sugar
> ½ cup (100 g) granulated sugar
> 1 egg
> 1 teaspoon vanilla extract
> 2½ cups (300 g) all-purpose flour
> ½ teaspoon baking soda
> ½ teaspoon salt
> ⅓ cup (79 mL) 2% or skim milk
> ½ package (12-ounce [341-g] size) semisweet chocolate morsels

1. Preheat the oven to 375°F (190°C). Grease cookie sheets.

2. Beat the butter and sugars in a medium bowl until fluffy; beat in the egg and vanilla. Mix in the combined flour, baking soda, and salt alternately with the milk, beginning and ending with the flour mixture. Mix in the chocolate morsels. Drop the dough by tablespoonfuls onto the prepared cookie sheets. Bake until browned, about 10 minutes. Cool on wire racks.

GLAZED CHOCOLATE SHORTBREAD SQUARES (LACTO-OVO)

Rich, chocolaty, and crisp!

5 DOZEN SQUARES

> 1½ cups (182 g) all-purpose flour
> ¼ cup (22 g) unsweetened cocoa powder
> ¾ cup (150 g) sugar
> ¼ teaspoon salt
> 8 tablespoons (112 g) cold butter or margarine
> 1 egg
> 2 teaspoons vanilla extract
> Sugar Glaze (recipe follows)

1. Preheat the oven to 350°F (180°C). Grease a 15 x 10-inch (37.5 x 25-cm) jelly-roll pan.

2. Combine the flour, cocoa, sugar, and salt in a medium bowl; cut in the butter with a pastry blender or 2 knives until mixture resembles coarse crumbs. Mix in the egg and vanilla, stirring just enough to form a soft dough. Pat the dough evenly into the prepared pan using fingers. Pierce dough with tines of fork.

3. Bake until firm to the touch, 20 to 25 minutes. Cool slightly on a wire rack. Spoon the Sugar Glaze over and cut into squares while warm.

SUGAR GLAZE

ABOUT 1 CUP (237 ML)

> 1 cup (100 g) confectioners' sugar
> 2–3 tablespoons 2% or skim milk

1.   Mix the powdered sugar with enough milk for desired consistency.

RAISIN OATMEAL COOKIES (LACTO-OVO)

Moist and chewy, just the way they should be!

2½ DOZEN COOKIES

> 6 tablespoons (84 g) butter or margarine, room temperature
> ¼ cup (59 mL) sour cream
> 1 egg
> 1 teaspoon vanilla extract
> 1 cup (225 g) packed light brown sugar
> 1½ cups (135 g) quick-cooking oats
> 1 cup (121 g) all-purpose flour
> ½ teaspoon baking soda
> ¼ teaspoon baking powder
> 1 teaspoon ground cinnamon
> ½ cup (83 g) raisins

1.   Preheat the oven to 350°F (180°C). Grease cookie sheets.

2.   Mix the butter, sour cream, egg, and vanilla in a large bowl; beat in the brown sugar. Mix in the combined oats, flour, baking soda, baking powder, and cinnamon. Mix in the raisins. Drop the dough onto the prepared cookie sheets, using 2 tablespoons for each cookie. Bake until cookies are browned, 12 to 15 minutes. Cool on wire racks.

CHOCOLATE BUTTERMILK CAKE WITH MOCHA FROSTING (LACTO-OVO) >

A chocolate dream come true, this cake is three layers high and generously covered with creamy mocha frosting!

16 SERVINGS

6 tablespoons (72 g) vegetable shortening
1 cup (200 g) granulated sugar
½ cup (113 g) packed light brown sugar
3 eggs
1 teaspoon vanilla extract
2 cups (212 g) cake flour
½ cup (43 g) unsweetened cocoa powder
2 teaspoons baking powder
½ teaspoon baking soda
½ teaspoon salt
1 cup (237 mL) buttermilk
Mocha Frosting (recipe follows)

1. Preheat the oven to 350°F (180°C). Grease and flour 3 (8-inch [20-cm]) round cake pans.

2. Beat the shortening, sugars, eggs, and vanilla in a large bowl until smooth. Mix in the combined flour, cocoa, baking powder, baking soda, and salt alternately with buttermilk, beginning and ending with the flour mixture. Pour batter into prepared pans.

3. Bake until toothpicks inserted into centers of cakes come out clean, 25 to 30 minutes. Cool in pans on wire racks 10 minutes; invert onto wire racks and cool.

4. Place 1 cake layer on a serving plate; frost with about ½ cup (119 mL) Mocha Frosting. Repeat with the second cake layer;

MOCHA FROSTING

ABOUT 2½ CUPS (593 ML)

> 5 cups (500 g) confectioners' sugar
> ½ cup (43 g) unsweetened cocoa powder
> 2–3 teaspoons instant coffee crystals
> 1 tablespoon butter or margarine, room temperature
> 1 teaspoon vanilla extract
> 4–5 tablespoons (60–75 mL) 2% or skim milk

1. Combine the powdered sugar, cocoa, coffee crystals, and butter in a large bowl; beat in the vanilla and enough milk to make the consistency spreadable.

CARROT CAKE WITH CREAM CHEESE FROSTING (LACTO-OVO)

Moist and sweetly spiced, this cake is one you'll want to make over and over again.

3 cups (330 g) shredded carrots

½ cup (83 g) raisins

1 cup (225 g) packed light brown sugar

⅓ cup (79 mL) vegetable oil

3 eggs

2 cups (242 g) all-purpose flour

1 teaspoon baking powder

1 teaspoon baking soda

1 teaspoon ground cinnamon

¼ teaspoon ground allspice

¼ teaspoon nutmeg

¼ teaspoon salt

Cream Cheese Frosting (recipe follows)

1. Preheat the oven to 350°F (180°C). Grease and flour two 8-inch (20-cm) round cake pans.

2. Mix the carrots, raisins, brown sugar, oil, and eggs in a large bowl. Mix in the combined flour, baking powder, baking soda, cinnamon, allspice, nutmeg, and salt. Pour into the prepared pans.

3. Bake until toothpicks inserted into cakes come out clean, 25 to 30 minutes. Cool in the pans on wire racks 10 minutes; remove from the pans.

4. Place 1 cake layer on a serving plate and frost with Cream Cheese Frosting. Top with the second cake layer, frosting the top and side of cake.

CREAM CHEESE FROSTING

ABOUT 3 CUPS (711 ML)

> 1 package (8 ounces [227 g]) Neufchatel or cream cheese, room temperature
> 2 tablespoons butter or margarine, room temperature
> 1 teaspoon vanilla extract
> 4–5 cups (400–500 g) confectioners' sugar

1. Beat the cream cheese, butter, and vanilla in a medium bowl until smooth; beat in enough confectioners' sugar to make the consistency spreadable.

CHOCOLATE–CHERRY PUDDING CAKE (LACTO)

Served warm, this fudgy favorite will bring smiles to kids of all ages.

14 SERVINGS

1¾ cups (212 g) all-purpose flour

1¼ cups (250 g) granulated sugar

⅓ cup (65 g) plus ¼ cup (22 g) unsweetened cocoa powder, divided

3 tablespoons baking powder

¾ cup (178 mL) 2% or skim milk

½ cup (172 g) unsweetened applesauce

1 cup (150 g) fresh, or frozen thawed, sweet cherries, pitted

¼ cup (27 g) chopped pecans

1¼ cups (281 g) packed dark brown sugar

3 cups (711 mL) hot water

1. Preheat the oven to 350°F (180°C). Grease and flour a 13 x 9-inch (32.5 x 22.5-cm) baking pan.

2. Combine the flour, granulated sugar, ⅓ cup (65 g) cocoa, and baking powder in a large bowl; stir in the milk and applesauce just until dry ingredients are moistened. Fold in the cherries and pecans. Spoon batter into the prepared pan. Mix the brown sugar, hot water, and ¼ cup (22 g) cocoa in a medium bowl until smooth; pour over the batter.

3. Bake 35 to 40 minutes or until set (cake will have a pudding-like texture). Serve warm or at room temperature.

BANANA–CINNAMON CAKE (LACTO-OVO)

Bananas add flavor and moistness to this picnic-perfect cake.

10 SERVINGS

> 1 package (6 ounces [170 g]) custard-style banana yogurt
> 1 cup (225 g) mashed ripe banana
> 2 tablespoons butter or margarine, room temperature
> 1 egg
> 1 teaspoon vanilla extract
> 1½ cups (182 g) all-purpose flour
> ½ cup (113 g) packed light brown sugar
> 2 teaspoons baking powder
> 1 teaspoon baking soda
> 1 teaspoon ground cinnamon
> ¼ teaspoon salt
> Confectioners' Sugar Frosting (recipe follows)

1. Preheat the oven to 375°F (180°C). Grease and flour a 9-inch (22.5-cm) baking pan.

2. Mix the yogurt, banana, butter, egg, and vanilla in a large bowl until smooth; mix in the flour, brown sugar, baking powder, baking soda, cinnamon, and salt. Pour into the prepared baking pan.

3. Bake 25 to 30 minutes or until the cake springs back when touched in the center. Cool in the pan on a wire rack 10 minutes; invert onto wire rack and cool.

4. Spread with Confectioners' Sugar Frosting.

CONFECTIONERS' SUGAR FROSTING

ABOUT ½ CUP (119 ML)

> 1 cup (100 g) confectioners' sugar
> 2 tablespoons butter or margarine, melted
> 2–3 tablespoons (30–45 mL) 2% or skim milk

1. Mix all the ingredients, adding enough milk to make spreadable consistency.

PINEAPPLE–LEMON TRIFLE (OVO)

Select your prettiest glass bowl for this attractive dessert. A fruit purée replaces the more traditional preserves, enhancing the use of fresh fruits in this recipe.

12 SERVINGS

> 1 package (18¼ ounces [518 g]) white cake mix
> 1½ cups (356 mL) water
> 3 egg whites
> 1½ cups (225 g) pineapple chunks in juice, drained
> Lemon Custard (recipe follows)
> 1 pint strawberries, sliced
> 2 medium bananas, sliced
> ¾ cup (178 mL) light non-dairy whipped topping

1. Preheat the oven to 350°F (180°C). Lightly grease and flour a 13 x 9-inch (32.5 x 22.5-cm) baking pan.

2. Prepare the cake mix according to package directions, using 1½ cups (356 mL) water and 3 egg whites. Pour into the prepared pan.

3. Bake 28 to 30 minutes, or until the cake springs back when touched. Cool on a wire rack. Cut half the cake into 1-inch (2.5-cm) cubes. (Reserve or freeze remaining cake for another use.)

4. Process the pineapple chunks in a blender or food processor until smooth. Layer ⅓ of the cake cubes in the bottom of a 2-quart (1.90-L) glass serving bowl. Spoon ⅓ of the Lemon Custard and pineapple purée over the cake cubes; top with ⅓ of the strawberries and bananas. Repeat the layers twice. Refrigerate until chilled, about 1 hour. Garnish with whipped topping.

LEMON CUSTARD

ABOUT 2 CUPS (474 ML)

¼ cup (50 g) sugar
2 tablespoons corn starch
2 tablespoons flour
1 cup (237 mL) 2% or skim milk
½ cup (119 mL) lemon juice
2 eggs, lightly beaten
¼ teaspoon ground nutmeg

1. Mix the sugar, corn starch, and flour in a medium saucepan; stir in the milk and lemon juice. Cook over medium heat, stirring, until the mixture boils and thickens, about 1 minute. Stir about ½ cup (119 mL) of the milk mixture into the eggs; stir the egg mixture back into the saucepan. Cook over low heat, stirring, 1 minute. Remove from the heat and cool; stir in the nutmeg. Refrigerate until chilled, 1 to 2 hours.

BANANAS FOSTER (LACTO)

A real taste of New Orleans!

4 SERVINGS

¼ cup (56 g) packed light brown sugar

1½ teaspoons corn starch

½ cup (119 mL) water

1 tablespoon rum or ½ teaspoon rum extract

1 teaspoon vanilla extract

2 medium bananas, sliced

¼ cup (25 g) toasted pecan halves

1⅓ cups (316 mL) vanilla ice cream

1. Mix the brown sugar and corn starch in a small saucepan; stir in the water and heat to boiling. Boil, stirring, until thickened, about 1 minute. Stir in the rum and vanilla; add bananas and simmer until hot, 1 to 2 minutes. Stir in the pecans; serve warm over ice cream.

CHOCOLATE PHYLLO CHEESECAKE (LACTO-OVO) >

Crisp, golden layers of phyllo make a delicate crust for this cheesecake.

12 SERVINGS

2 tablespoons unseasoned dry bread crumbs

6 sheets frozen phyllo pastry, thawed

Vegetable cooking spray

3 packages (8 ounces [227 g] each) Neufchatel or cream cheese, room temperature

1 cup (237 mL) sour cream

⅔ cup (134 g) sugar

⅓ cup (29 g) Dutch process cocoa powder

2 eggs

3 tablespoons (23 g) all-purpose flour

½ teaspoon ground cinnamon

1. Preheat the oven to 375°F (190°C). Grease a 9-inch (22.5-cm) springform pan.

2. Coat the prepared pan with bread crumbs. Spray each phyllo sheet lightly with cooking spray. Layer phyllo in the bottom of the pan, turning each sheet slightly so that corners are staggered. Bake until lightly browned, 6 to 8 minutes. Cool on a wire rack.

3. Reduce oven temperature to 350°F (180°C). Beat the cream cheese in a large bowl until fluffy; mix in the sour cream, sugar, and cocoa. Beat in the eggs; mix in the flour and cinnamon. Pour into the phyllo crust; gently fold sides of phyllo inward so they do not extend beyond the edge of the pan.

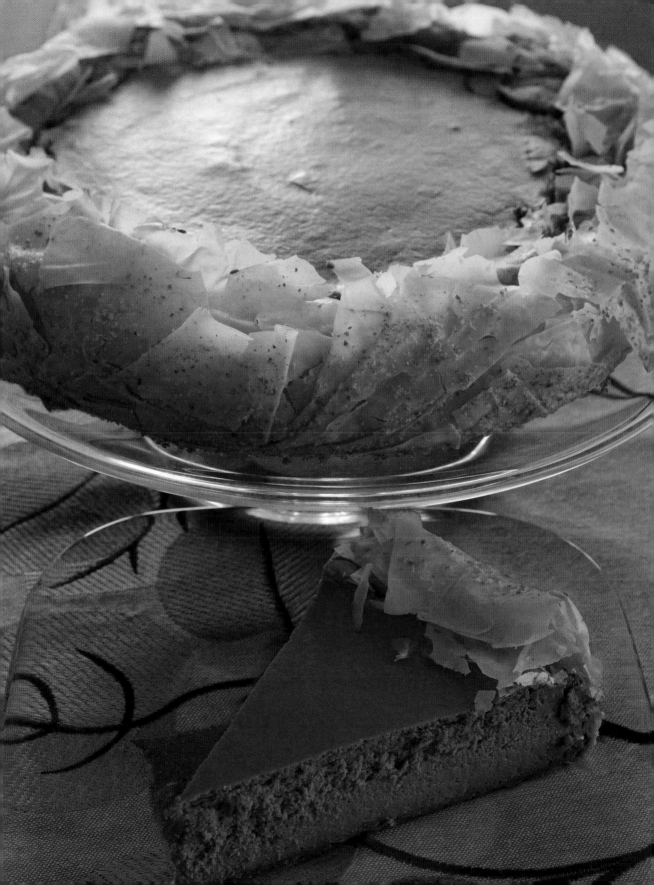

4. Bake until the cheesecake is set, but still slightly soft in the center, about 50 minutes. Cover the edge of the phyllo crust with foil during the last 15 or 20 minutes of baking time, if they begin to get too brown.

5. Cool on a wire rack 10 minutes. Carefully loosen the side of the pan; cool to room temperature. Cover loosely and refrigerate 8 hours or overnight.

INDEX

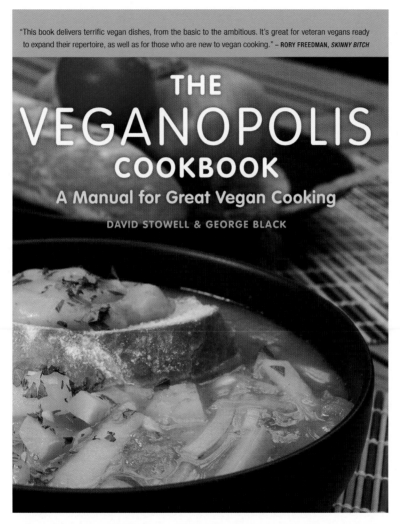

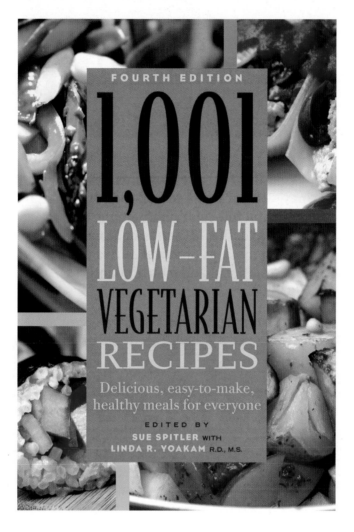

ABOUT THE SERIES

Each of the books in the *101* series features delicious, diverse, and accessible recipes—101 of them, to be exact. Scattered throughout each book are beautiful full-color photographs to show you just what the dish should look like. The *101* series books also feature a simple, contemporary design that's as practical as it is elegant, with measures calculated in both traditional and metric quantities.

ABOUT THE EDITOR

Perrin Davis is co-editor of Surrey's *101* series. She lives with her family in suburban Chicago.